The 12-Week DBT Plan

The 12-Week DBT PLAN

Skills and Exercises to Improve Your *Feelings, Habits,* and *Relationships*

Valerie Dunn McBee, LCSW

callisto publishing
an imprint of Sourcebooks

Art Directors: Michael Cook and Lisa Schreiber

Art Producers: Maya Melenchuk and Stacey Stambaugh

Editor: John Makowski and Adrian Potts

Production Editor: Jenna Dutton and Rachel Taenzler

Production Manager: Jose Olivera and Martin Worthington

Published by Callisto Publishing LLC C/O Sourcebooks LLC

P.O. Box 4410, Naperville, Illinois 60567-4410

(630) 961-3900

callistopublishing.com

Originally published as *The 12-Week DBT Workbook: Practical Dialectical Behavior Therapy Skills to Regain Emotional Stability* in 2022 in the United States of America by Callisto Publishing, an imprint of Callisto Publishing LLC. This edition based on the paperback published in 2022 in the United States of America by Callisto Publishing, an imprint of Callisto Publishing LLC.

Printed in the United States of America

For my Oren, Judah, and Ariela, who keep me centered; my parents, who were stellar examples of dialectical tension leading to good things; and my clients, who allow me to walk with them.

Contents

Introduction

You may have picked up this book because the cover caught your eye, or you're interested in self-improvement or the world of psychology. Perhaps you're feeling like some things in your life aren't quite the way you want them to be. Maybe you're curious about what exactly DBT is and how it might help you.

Dialectical behavior therapy (DBT) is a therapy that was designed for people with significant struggles with emotions and behaviors, but the skills in DBT are skills that all people can benefit from. We all have emotions, relationships, problems that need to be solved, and stressors to contend with, and we all can benefit from learning to stay present in our lives. These are life skills for everyone, not just tools for "people with problems."

This is one of the reasons I love DBT: It's practical and it doesn't set people in therapy apart from other people. As a therapist who loves the process, the journey, the insights, and the "aha" moments, my enthusiasm for the structure of DBT is a bit surprising. If you had told me at the beginning of my career that I would become a behavioral therapist providing structured, action-driven therapy, I would probably not have believed you. Here we are, 17 years later, and I—the reluctant behaviorist—am here to stay.

I'm a huge fan of evidence-based therapies and practices. Evidence-based means extensive research has shown that a consistently provided intervention produces consistently effective results. Simply put, I ended up here because DBT works and the proof, as they say, is in the pudding of changed lives and relief from suffering.

While I can't be in the therapy room with you, my goal with this book is to make the life-changing tools of DBT affordable and accessible to everyone—patients, clinicians, and curious readers alike—providing you with an informative overview of what DBT is, what it's used for, and how it can be used to help heal and manage symptoms for a variety of different disorders. Wherever you are on your journey, this interactive workbook should provide you with the foundation you need to establish a DBT skills practice. Whether you're a client, a therapist, or just a person hoping for something better, I hope you can find something good and useful in these pages.

How to Use This Book

The purpose of this book is to provide you with skills and techniques to move you toward emotional balance and freedom so you can live life on your terms rather than feeling controlled by your emotions. The book is organized as a 12-week plan so you can move at a comfortable pace, without feeling overwhelmed. The skills in these pages are not a replacement for comprehensive DBT, but they are a key piece of DBT and have the potential to be extremely helpful on their own.

The first few chapters of this workbook give you some background on DBT and its aims and structure, as well as a few tips for using the book effectively. The remaining chapters present the skills themselves, as well as exercises for you to practice in your daily life, with written exercises to complete either in the workbook itself or in your designated DBT journal.

You will spend three weeks in mindfulness, three in distress tolerance, three in emotion regulation, and the final three in interpersonal effectiveness. Together, these modules will increase your ability to stay present in the moment; get through a crisis without making it worse; fully experience, regulate, and respond rather than react to your emotions; and be more effective at getting what you want and need in relationships. Feel free to refer back to specific skills and exercises as often as needed.

AN IMPORTANT SAFETY REMINDER

This point will be reiterated later in the book, but it is important enough to mention twice. Many of the patterns and behaviors that people who come to DBT are dealing with can be dangerous and life-threatening. Suicidality and self-harm are common to our folks in DBT, and while we are not afraid to address these topics, we also don't take them lightly. If you find that you are struggling with thoughts of wanting to harm yourself or end your life, this book is likely not going to provide enough support for you right now. If you are in immediate danger, please seek emergency services (911) or call the National Suicide Prevention Lifeline at 1-800-273-TALK (8255). I also encourage you to use the Resources in the back of this book (page 164) to help you find a qualified DBT therapist to walk with you through this process. There is hope, and we can help.

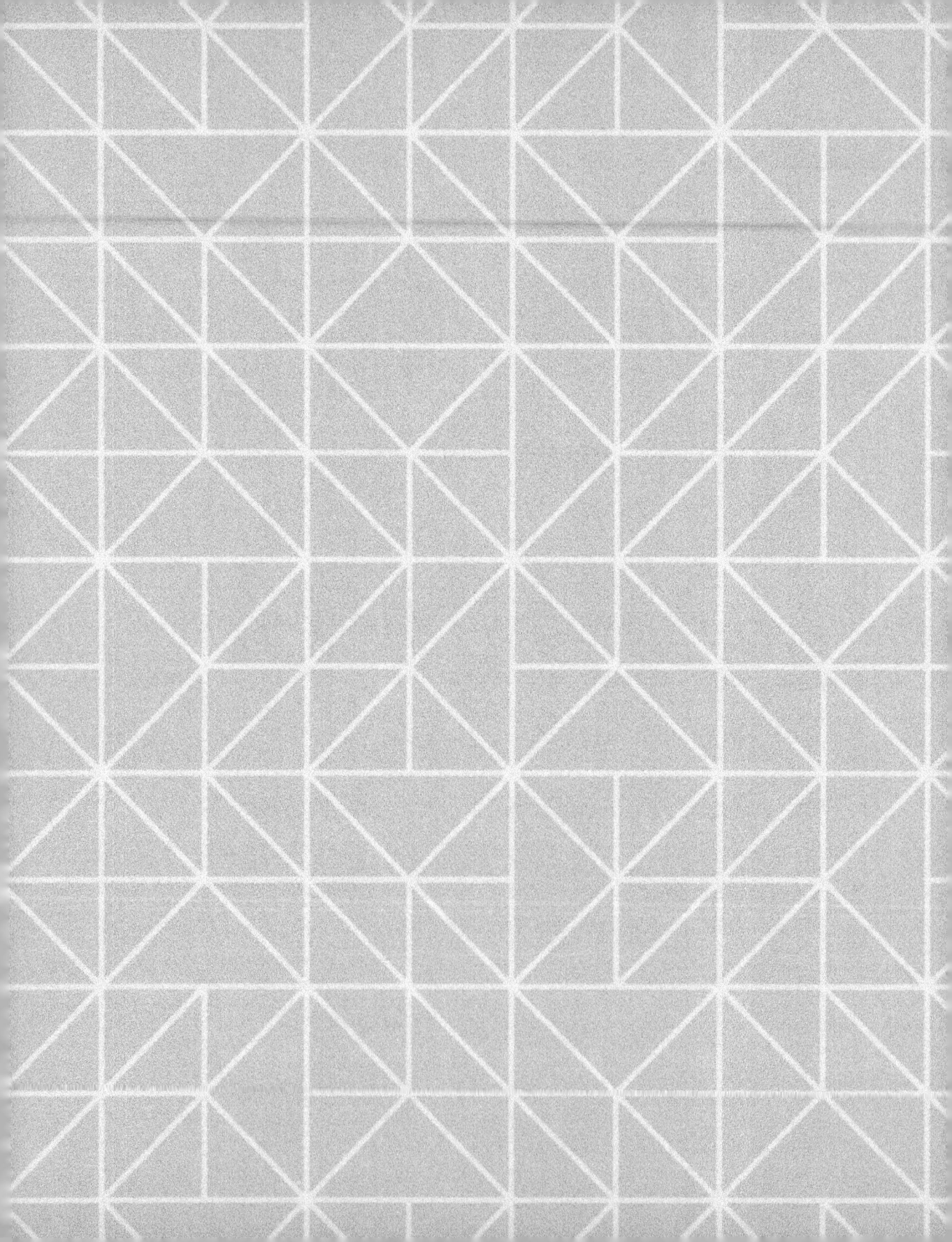

Before You Get Started

When people start DBT, the first few sessions are referred to as *pre-treatment*. During this time, they learn what DBT is about and how we approach problems in DBT. They also identify their goals and targets for therapy before making a commitment to fully engage in the process. You might consider part 1 of this book to be your pre-treatment. You will learn about the foundations of DBT and the way we conceptualize and approach problems. Then you can decide whether you are ready to commit to the process and set yourself up for success with some tips provided. I hope you'll stay.

CHAPTER 1

Understanding DBT

*Tension is uncomfortable,
but balance doesn't exist without it.*

In this chapter, I give you a bit of background on what DBT is, specifically what the *D* in DBT stands for. I will also give some brief explanations of the skills modules that make up the bulk of this book. While it's impossible to fully explain DBT within the confines of a workbook, I'm hoping to give you a sense of where it came from and why it is so profound, and to give you a sense of the hope that it can provide when things seem hopeless.

WHAT IS DBT?

Dialectical behavior therapy (DBT) is an adaptation of Aaron Beck's cognitive behavioral therapy (CBT), the basic premise of which is that in order to change our behaviors, we need to identify and change the thoughts, feelings, and beliefs that lead to the behaviors. DBT recognizes the value and importance of changing behaviors but also recognizes that certain patterns of behaviors are extremely difficult to change and need specialized attention.

When Dr. Marsha Linehan was first developing DBT at the University of Washington in the 1980s, she recognized that for people with really big, over-whelming emotions, it was even more difficult to change some of the ways that they had learned to cope with a life of big emotions. She noticed that if the focus of therapy was largely on the need to change, people often felt that they were being blamed for their problems. On the other hand, if there was too much emphasis on acceptance and understanding, people felt that no one understood how miserable they were and how desperate they were for things to improve. Linehan realized that there needed to be a balance of acceptance *and* change.

With the goal of building a life that each individual experiences as worth living, the tension of acceptance and change moves DBT participants along that path. Some of the tools used along the way are behavior tracking and analysis, validation, cognitive modification, emotion exposure, problem-solving, contingency management, and skill building, the last of which we will focus on in this book. These are all clinical ways of saying that when we are trying to change, we will use everything in our arsenal to try to shift our thoughts, emotions, and ways of coping to move us toward emotional freedom.

DBT was originally designed to treat borderline personality disorder, chronic suicidality, and self-harm. It has since been adapted and proven effective for many issues, including depression, mood disorders, attention-deficit/hyperactivity disorder (ADHD), post-traumatic stress disorder (PTSD), eating disorders, substance use disorders, and more. Research trials over the last 30-plus years have shown that DBT is effective for a variety of issues with a hallmark of challenges in regulating emotions. DBT has also been studied across racial, ethnic, and cultural populations, and research supports DBT being effective across age, gender, and sexual orientation. The skills are useful for all humans.

The Four Core Principles of DBT

As DBT was developing, it became apparent that certain behavioral patterns or skills deficits are common to many people, and that in order to change, people need to learn new skills in all relevant areas of their lives. DBT is organized into four core principals or skills modules—mindfulness, distress tolerance, emotion regulation, and interpersonal effectiveness. Each skills module is designed to address categories of deficits:

PROBLEMS TO DECREASE	MODULE
Problems with focus, awareness, and confusion; staying present	Mindfulness
Impulsivity, escaping, or avoiding emotions through problem behaviors	Distress tolerance
Big emotions, mood changes, and negative emotional states	Emotion regulation
Difficulty keeping relationships, fulfilling wants/needs, and maintaining self-respect	Interpersonal effectiveness

While undertaking the work of skills training, it is essential for both clinicians and patients to understand the following assumptions of DBT:

1. People are doing the best that they can.

2. People want to improve.

3. People must learn new behaviors in all relevant contexts.

4. People cannot fail in DBT.

5. People may not have caused all their problems, but they have to solve them anyway.

6. People need to do better, try harder, and be more motivated to change.

7. The lives of people who are suicidal feel unbearable as they are currently being lived.

Sometimes when people begin to learn the skills, they are not sure what to make of acronyms such as STOP, TIP, ABC PLEASE, DEAR MAN, and others. The acronyms can even make some people feel they're being talked down to. Please know that the acronyms themselves are just teaching tools; they are not the skills themselves. As she was developing DBT, Linehan spent time finding out what therapists were teaching their clients to help with particular challenges, gathered as many techniques as she could find, and then packaged them into skills in these teachable formats.

Where we know the specific background of skills, such as the Zen or Buddhist roots of mindfulness, I have given that background. The rest are a tried and tested group of accumulated skills that we know work.

Mindfulness

Mindfulness is an ancient practice that is historically associated with Buddhism. Similar practices can be seen in almost every spiritual tradition. In DBT, it is scientific mindfulness that is the focus. Mindfulness can be conceptualized as the thread that weaves the other DBT skills together. Simply put, mindfulness is the practice of being able to notice your thoughts, and then choosing what you are paying attention to at any given moment and staying present in that moment. Many people who have dealt with overwhelming emotions find this concept revolutionary—that we can learn to have a choice about what our brain is focusing on in difficult moments.

Distress Tolerance

What is the difference between stress and distress? *Stress* is difficult but generally manageable. *Distress*, on the other hand, is overwhelming. Usually, the emotional and logical parts of the brain function like a fulcrum. Sometimes one is more in control than the other, but generally they balance each other out. Sometimes, though, one part or the other is calling the shots. When the emotional brain is overwhelmed, the logical part goes off-line, which leads to emotional crisis. The two types of distress-tolerance skills—crisis survival and reality acceptance—can help us get through a crisis without making it worse

Emotion Regulation

The difficulty with having big emotions is not the emotions themselves; it's not having the skills to regulate or balance them. It can feel like they are driving the car, so to speak. Linehan's biosocial theory, part of the basis for DBT, suggests that people who experience patterns of overwhelming emotion have a biological predisposition toward them. This shows up as high sensitivity (big, intense emotions), high reactivity (big response), and slow return to baseline. These characteristics are not always problematic on their own, but they can be extremely problematic when a person does not learn the skills needed to regulate them.

Interpersonal Effectiveness

One area of life that can be strongly impacted by overwhelming emotions is relationships. Many challenges can come up when a person struggles to manage their emotions, and it is not uncommon for there to be a strong, history-based fear that people will get tired of the individual and leave. The interpersonal effectiveness module centers on choosing our priorities in interactions with others: our objective, the relationship, or our self-respect. Knowing the priority going into an interaction can help us decide how to be effective in either asking for what we need or saying no to someone else's request.

THE THEORY OF DIALECTICS

Foundational to the way we think in DBT is the concept of dialectics. A *dialectic* is a philosophy term that means to hold seemingly opposing ideas in tension. Most things in life are not either/or equations, but rather, both/and situations. In DBT, the main dialectic that drives the work is acceptance and change: You are doing the best you can. Period. *And* you need to work harder to solve all your problems that are within your ability to solve.

Being in a DBT session is like dancing, weaving together validation (acknowledgment and acceptance that whatever you're experiencing makes sense if you understand how you got there) and push for change (the ways you've been coping may not be working so well, or at least aren't enough to move you forward to get the life you want). There are three premises that are part of dialectical thinking: finding truth in opposites, understanding that reality is continuously changing, and becoming aware of the interconnectedness of everything.

Finding Truth in Opposites

Most things are made up of opposites. Things, or people, can get "stuck" when a synthesis can't be reached between those opposites. DBT expert Charlie Swenson likens it to the steadfastness of a logjam. For folks who live in extremes and tend toward polarized or rigid thinking, it can be difficult to think dialectically or to balance opposites, or to get out of a logjam. Some common examples of dialectical thinking are:

- I'm upset with you, and I still love you.
- I want to live in the moment, and I am making plans for the future.
- I can see where you're coming from, and I have a different opinion.
- I'm doing the best I can, and I need to try harder and do better.
- This frustrating thing that happened feels huge but hasn't ruined my whole day.

Without being able to embrace the truth of both sides, a person can be stuck feeling like they can't solve the problem or move forward. If we can sit with this tension, we can keep and improve upon the core of validity in both views, arriving at a new way of seeing things.

Reality Is Continuously Changing

Nothing stays the same. Every aspect of every context you can imagine is in flux. Even things that seem absolutely stuck and unchanging are changing, though perhaps slowly. People change, buildings that seem permanent change, mountains and oceans change. Another way to say this is that we are in a continuous process of change. Often it can seem like the behaviors and feelings we are addressing in therapy will never shift. Eventually, though, they will. It is in the nature of all things. We may keep asking the question "What am I missing?" Sometimes we find what we are missing and that leads to change. Other times while we are waiting to figure it out, some aspect of a situation will shift separately from our efforts, and that will create the space needed for recognizable change. Even in situations where it seems impossible, we maintain hope and keep trying, knowing that it is the nature of things to change.

The Interconnectedness of Everything

We are all connected. Who we are; what we think, feel, and experience; and our choices and lives are all influenced by the people and circumstances around us. There is not a person alive whose sense of self hasn't been influenced by the people they've encountered. This way of thinking comes from what we call a *systems perspective*. Each part of a system is a piece of the whole. You must understand the whole to understand each part. If one part shifts, it changes the whole system, and vice versa. This shows up in several ways in DBT. If you're struggling to change a problem or behavior directly, shifting another aspect of the system can produce change. Changing dynamics, such as in a family, provides space for an individual to change. It's not always easy for us to accept this, but it is part of life that we are both products of and contributors to our environment.

KEY TAKEAWAYS ·

With a brief look at what DBT is and where it came from, you now have some idea of how the skills in this book are designed to help you. You've also been introduced to the idea of dialectics. Trying to understand dialectics can be a bit tricky until you see the concepts in action, but as you start to notice the discomfort of thinking only in black and white, you will begin to see the value.

Key points from this chapter:

▸ We all need skills in all areas of our lives, and we are capable of learning new things.

▸ Emotions are important, but we don't want them driving the bus.

▸ Tension is uncomfortable, but it can lead to growth.

▸ Change will come.

CHAPTER 2

Beginning Your DBT Practice

Change is hard; having a plan helps.
Seeing others who have succeeded
can inspire you to keep trying.

In this chapter, I will give you a bit more information about the structure of DBT. I will include the four modes, or ingredients, of treatment, as well as the five functions or aims of the therapy. It may seem like information that you don't really need to know, but understanding the way DBT is structured can help us wrap our heads around the specific approaches to building skills, and how they are meant to help. At the end of the chapter, we will look at some ideas for how you can set yourself up for success as you dive into this workbook and into improving your life.

THE FOUR MODES OF TREATMENT

There are four modes of treatment that must be present for a program to call itself *adherent DBT*. These modes are group skills training, individual therapy, phone skills coaching, and therapist consultation teams. While this book focuses on the development of skills, I will briefly describe the functions of all four modes.

Group Skills Training

One of the seven assumptions about DBT clients mentioned in chapter 1 is that they need to learn new skills in all relevant areas of life. Research indicates that if a person has access to only one aspect of DBT, skills training is the mode that can be most effective as a stand-alone. In traditional DBT programs, this would be done in a group setting. The skills curriculum provides training in four major categories that will be discussed at length in this workbook: mindfulness, distress tolerance, emotion regulation, and interpersonal effectiveness. Each set of skills is designed to teach effective ways to cope in areas where there are often struggles or deficits, as detailed in chapter 1. They are divided between skills that help us accept our current reality and skills that help us make things better. Together, they help make a life that can sometimes feel intolerable more bearable. These skills aren't just helpful for people with "emotional problems." These are skills that we all need to live our lives well.

Individual Therapy

Individual therapy in DBT is the place where participants can really dig into their own goals and targets. It is more structured than traditional talk therapy, with a focus on tracking, analyzing, accepting/validating, and changing emotional and behavioral patterns. Because the goal of DBT is to get to a life you experience as worth living, there is a focus on understanding and managing emotions and behaviors with the intention of removing obstacles to getting that life.

The priority order in which we address targets is:

1. Life-threatening behaviors—to keep you alive

2. Therapy-interfering behaviors—to keep you in therapy

3. Quality-of-life-interfering behaviors—to solve problems that are keeping you from the life you want

In the context of a trusting relationship with the therapist, clients build skills and remove the barriers to a life worth living.

Phone Skills Coaching

When clients are in DBT and have made a commitment to taking suicidality and self-harm off the table, they have access to their therapist around the clock. If clients find themselves in difficult situations and need support to either stay safe or to be skillful, they can reach out to their therapist via phone or text for skills suggestions. Parameters for using phone coaching appropriately include:

▸ Hitting Send on the text or call equals a commitment to staying safe and skillful.
▸ Phone coaching is not extra therapy; it is skills support.
▸ If a client refuses to be skillful, they don't have access to phone coaching.

Phone coaching helps reduce crisis and increase skillfulness throughout the week and not just in the therapy room.

Therapist Consultation Team

This is an aspect of DBT that a client does not see, but it is a crucial and non-negotiable component of the treatment. If a therapist is not part of a DBT consultation team, then it's not adherent DBT.

The team serves several purposes:

▸ Supports therapists in staying adherent to the model
▸ Increases the therapist's skill and motivation
▸ Provides therapy for the therapists

In DBT, we are working on behaviors and emotions that can be extremely difficult to change. It can be stressful work, so having the support and encouragement of a team is crucial to reducing burnout. The client may not witness the functioning of the team, but they benefit from it immensely. They're thought to be the client of the whole team and the whole team is invested in the client's progress and well-being.

THE FIVE FUNCTIONS OF TREATMENT

This book is based on Linehan's model of DBT. In the field, we call it *full* or *comprehensive DBT*. What this means is that all four of the previously discussed modes are part of the program. If one of the modes is missing, it is simply not considered comprehensive or adherent DBT. That is not to say that individual aspects of DBT can't be helpful, such as the skills presented in this book. Any program claiming to offer full DBT, though, must include the following five crucial functions. Each aspect of the treatment is included, because over the 40+ years that the treatment has been in development and use, research and trials have shown that it is the combination of these approaches that nets the greatest results. There are many aspects of DBT that are flexible, but these functions are the core of the treatment and as such are necessary.

Increasing Your Motivation to Change

Clients increase their motivation to change primarily in the context of individual therapy. This happens through tracking emotions and behaviors on a diary card and using chain analysis to understand the factors that are keeping them stuck in the old, ineffective behaviors. Other ways of increasing motivation are exposure/practicing tolerating uncomfortable emotions and rewarding desired new behaviors. As people learn that they can both tolerate emotions and begin to choose new and more effective ways of coping, their motivation to continue increases.

Learning new things is challenging, and so is letting go of the familiar. It is a common experience for people to recognize the need to change but to still cling to the comfort and familiarity of their old ways of coping, sometimes even digging in their heels and refusing to try new things. Helping people get to the point where they recognize the need to change—by building their confidence so they understand it is worth the effort to try—is a key function of the treatment and happens most in individual therapy.

Enhancing Your Capabilities

One of the assertions of DBT is that people in DBT need to learn new behaviors and skills in all relevant contexts in life. Learning these new skills will enhance one's capabilities to respond more effectively to all of life's challenges. This includes the skills taught in the modules of DBT: mindfulness, emotion regulation, distress tolerance, and interpersonal effectiveness. In adolescent and multifamily DBT, there is additional material on walking the middle path, or finding dialectical balance in family relationships. Further enhancement of skills happens through role-plays, activities, group discussion, practice, homework, rehearsal, and phone coaching.

Generalizing What You've Learned for Life

It is not assumed that a skill learned in the therapy room will automatically be accessible in other contexts. In order to be sure that clients are able to use the skills learned in everyday life, we use homework, real-life practice, and phone coaching throughout the week. Some clients even record therapy sessions during the week to review and study later.

Research and experience seem to indicate that what we call *generalization of knowledge*, or the ability to transfer knowledge to new situations, is especially challenging when people deal with emotional and interpersonal dysregulation. Having support, via phone coaching, in managing and decreasing the dysregulation and calling to mind skills that are more effective helps people bring the new knowledge to mind outside of therapy.

Increasing Your Therapist's Motivation and Competence

DBT can be a challenging treatment to provide, as some of the issues clients are trying to address are stressful. Consistently dealing with life-threatening behaviors and emotional crises can lead to therapist burnout without enough support. Therapists stay on track and receive needed support through supervision, ongoing training, books and manuals, and weekly consultation teams, which all help them keep fidelity to the model of DBT.

There is also a community of DBT therapists around the world who are incredibly generous with their knowledge and experience. The ability to talk to other therapists who are treating similar issues and helping clients solve problems is invaluable. Many of the explanations and words in this book come out of the interactions in the DBT therapist community.

Restructuring Your Environment

As people are building new skills and learning to live the life they want, sometimes there are dynamics in their environments that make change and growth difficult. Shifting the environment to create a better chance for positive change could include interventions with the person's partner, family, or community, or it could include case management or coordination with other providers. The goal is to increase the likelihood that the person is reinforced for the new, effective behaviors and not the old, ineffective ones.

The preferred way to solve problems from a DBT perspective is to help the individual advocate for change in their own life. However, there are times when it makes sense for the therapist to get directly involved, perhaps in the context of case management or contact with other providers to coordinate care.

SETTING YOURSELF UP FOR SUCCESS

Most of us have heard the assertion that it takes 21 days to form a new habit. While there is debate about whether that's true or a myth, it is clear in experience and research from multiple directions that consistent practice is required to learn something new. Research even indicates that the mental practice of a task (i.e., walking through the steps in your mind) increases our physical abilities, and this has been demonstrated from surgeons to athletes in various studies. For example, a tennis player who mentally practices their serve actually performs it better.

As you start this workbook, be prepared to practice the skills often. The more you practice them when you're not in crisis, the more likely they will be to come to mind when you're struggling. There are also suggestions throughout the book to approach some of the exercises with caution. Addressing your emotions and behaviors can be challenging and sometimes overwhelming. Give yourself permission to go at your own pace and to seek support if it would be helpful. That said, I do encourage you to keep going even if you need to take breaks. Find the middle ground between avoiding and overdoing it.

Creating a DBT Notebook

There will be some space in this book for recording your responses to the skills exercises. I'd also encourage you to add a notebook to record your experiences as you go along. The more intentional and committed you are, the more you will learn. You can choose any type of notebook you like. Let it be useful and don't put too much pressure on yourself to make it perfect. It's for you and no one else.

Each day you are working on skills, write down a few essentials:

▶ Specific emotions that you're experiencing that day.

▶ Rate the emotion from 0 to 10.

▶ Rate the emotion after practicing a skill.

From there, the options are endless. You can describe and reflect on your emotions/behaviors, explore your thoughts about the skills, write what's on your mind, or draw your feelings. The goal is to have a record of your process so you can see the progress you're making.

When to Seek Professional Guidance

As previously mentioned, some of the challenges people are dealing with can feel overwhelming. The skills in this book can, over time, be helpful to you. If your challenges are dangerous or life-threatening, there is absolutely zero shame in recognizing you could benefit from professional support as you work through your struggles. Lifelong habits and patterns absolutely can change, but it can be extremely difficult. Let a professional walk through it with you.

If you're questioning whether you need professional guidance, here are some things to consider:

▶ Am I having thoughts of harming myself or others that I can't seem to shake?

▶ Am I unsure if I can keep myself safe?

▶ Am I doing things that are putting me at risk or making things worse?

▶ Have I been trying hard for a long time and things aren't getting better?

If you answered yes to any of these questions, please consider getting connected with a DBT clinician.

How to Find the Right DBT Clinician

There are a variety of ways to find a DBT clinician, including several online sources listed in the Resources section in the back of the book (page 164).

More important, how do you find the right therapist for you? If you are simply looking for someone who has a basic understanding of DBT skills, there are many therapists who will fit the bill. However, if you are looking for a highly specialized and trained DBT therapist who can provide comprehensive DBT, you will need to find a DBT center or provider who is part of what is called an *intensively trained team*. You can simply ask the person if they are part of a DBT team that is intensively trained. Behavioral Tech, Linehan's organization, also has a "Find a Therapist" option, as does the DBT-Linehan Board of Certification, which lists the mostly highly trained DBT therapists.

KEY TAKEAWAYS ·······························

You now have some understanding of the ways DBT can help you build skills so that you can get to a life that you experience as worth living. You also have an inkling of how to approach learning and practicing skills, and I hope you're planning to get, or already have, a dedicated notebook for your DBT work.

Key points from this chapter:

▸ The goals of DBT are to keep you alive and in therapy so that you can get the life you want.

▸ DBT therapists are highly trained to walk through this process with you, but the skills can make a difference even without a therapist.

▸ If you are actively suicidal, seek out a DBT therapist so you don't have to do this alone.

▸ You can set yourself up for success.

PART 2

Your 12-Week Plan

Now that you've gotten a bit of background on DBT and have some ideas for setting yourself up to practice and learn the skills, we will dive into the skills themselves. We will start with an exploration of mindfulness. This is the most conceptual module and can sometimes be challenging to wrap your head around. As you begin to engage with the exercises, though, my hope is that you will begin to see how truly practical mindfulness skills are and how helpful they can be.

Following mindfulness, we will spend three weeks in each of the other modules: learning about managing distress or crisis, regulating our emotions, and finally, learning to effectively ask for what we need in our relationships.

Ready to be skillful?

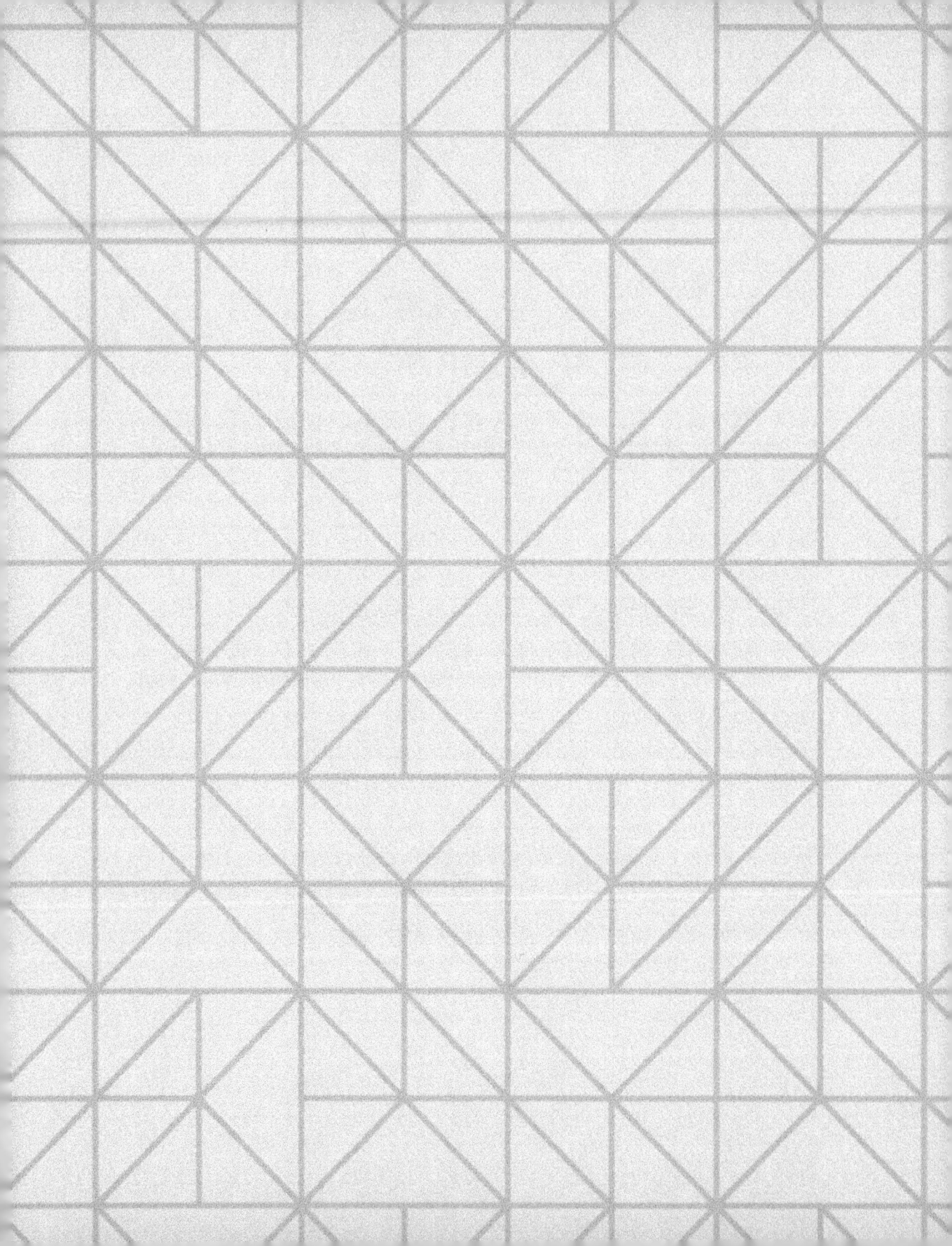

Exploring Your Mind with Mindfulness

Would you rather be able to control your mind or have your mind control you?

In this chapter, you will learn about the background and basic premises of mindfulness and how it came to be a part of DBT. You'll learn what its goals are and how mindfulness can improve your life. Hopefully, you'll begin to have a picture of why mindfulness is such an integral part of a therapy designed to help people pursue a meaningful life.

We'll not only discuss what mindfulness is, but we'll also learn about four types of mindfulness and be introduced to our ultimate goal in mindfulness: wise mind, the place where we find the balance between our emotional and reasonable, or rational, states of mind.

WHAT IS MINDFULNESS?

Mindfulness is quite the buzzword these days. You hear about it in business, health and fitness, and school curriculums. Claims suggest it reduces stress, anxiety, and depression; increases focus; improves sleep; and boosts immunity. For some it's a spiritual path, while others seek brain health. Others think it's just a fad or passing trend.

Dr. Marsha Linehan, influenced by Zen Buddhism, incorporated scientific mindfulness, or the mindfulness that scientists have studied and determined is effective separate from religious practice, into DBT. She decided on this rather than traditional meditation because so many of the people she was treating couldn't tolerate focusing on their breath and internal experience in meditation at the beginning of therapy. She was the first to officially incorporate mindfulness into psychotherapy, conceptualizing it as a foundation for the other skills.

Mindfulness, simply put, is choosing to pay attention to the present moment, as it is, without judging or trying to change it. Mindfulness practice can reduce suffering, increase happiness, increase control of your mind, and help you be present in your own life and to other people.

The Three States of Mind

Central to DBT's approach to mindfulness is the concept of Wise Mind. This is a dialectical practice that teaches us to access our innate inner wisdom through the integration of the opposing forces of our emotional and reasonable/rational states of mind. In the following section, we'll learn about each of those states of mind.

The Emotion Mind

Our emotion mind is the part of us where our emotions, interpretations, sensations, judgments, passions, and fears live. Emotions can motivate really important action, such as great bravery or great love. If we are functioning out of our emotion mind, our decisions and actions are determined solely by how we are feeling in the moment, often excluding factual thinking. Acting from emotion mind often has short-term benefits but long-term consequences. It's important to note that being highly emotional is not necessarily emotion mind. Emotion mind is when the emotions are in control of decisions.

The Reasonable Mind

Our reasonable, or rational, mind is clinical and detached, and focused on the facts to the exclusion of emotional concerns as well as our values. In reasonable mind, we can plan and evaluate logically. Reason is necessary but alone can be problematically dismissive of human connection. It doesn't attend to things like warmth, friendliness, and consideration of others' feelings and experiences. Functioning primarily in reasonable mind can therefore make it difficult to maintain relationships. Our emotions also don't get the attention they need when we suppress them in favor of only reason.

The Wise Mind

We all have a wise mind. No one is in wise mind all the time, but we each have built-in internal wisdom at the intersection of our emotional and reasonable minds. It's the part of you that can find truth or might be thought of as your "gut" or intuition. For many of us, it can be difficult to find, and accessing it will take practice.

Wise mind is a state of mind but also a practical skill. Practicing the skill will help you learn to access the state of mind. First, let's look at the practical skill.

MAKING A WISE-MINDED DECISION

For this exercise, think of a decision you're trying to make. On the left, write down facts and observations under "Reasonable Mind." On the right, note your emotions, fears, interpretations, judgments, and worries under "Emotion Mind." Then, taking into consideration both lists, you will write your wise-minded action in the center column under "Wise Mind."

As an example, let's say we're trying to decide whether to go to a wedding, knowing someone we don't like will be there. (Note: There is not one right answer here.)

REASONABLE MIND	WISE MIND	EMOTION MIND
Observing that I have many emotions and thoughts about this	I care more about the friends getting married than my dislike for the person I don't like. I will show up at the wedding with other friends who are supportive and will help keep me distracted. I will find other things to do so I don't focus on that person. It's okay that I don't want to be around them, so I will just try not to engage but focus on the wedding. I can even step outside if it gets difficult.	Feeling fear
Aware that friends want me there		Feeling worry
There will be many people there, only one of whom I dislike		Feeling sadness
Reason for going is love for friends		Wanting to avoid
Not sleeping		Worrying I'll be judged
Observing that I'm ruminating		Worried because I can't sleep

Give it a try with your own situation below or on a separate piece of paper.

Situation: ....

REASONABLE MIND	WISE MIND	EMOTION MIND

Exploring Your Own Mind

For many who have struggled with overwhelming emotions, difficult thoughts, and troubling behaviors, the prospect of exploring one's own mind may seem daunting or even scary. But the more you practice being aware of your inner world and listening to your wise mind, the more intuitive it will become. Initially, it can be difficult to recognize the difference between wise mind and a strong feeling. You can think of wise mind as the place where your well connects to the groundwater; it takes practice and determination to get past the barriers that you previously thought were the bottom of the well, but with commitment you will find that your well goes far deeper than you ever imagined. Initially, it will take careful consideration and analysis to determine whether you're in wise mind. Eventually, it will become easier to access and recognize.

LEARNING TO HEAR WISE MIND

There are many ways to practice accessing wise mind. It will take time to learn to recognize the difference between wise mind and reasonable or emotional mind. Learning to sit and listen, even when there isn't an immediate answer, will help you find that place of balance. Here are a few ways to try:

1. Breathe deeply. Pause at the top of the inhale and the bottom of the exhale. Focus your attention on being present in those pauses.

2. Breathing slowly, say the word "wise" to yourself as you inhale, then say "mind" as you exhale. Continue this pattern.

3. Practice asking wise mind a question that you're trying to find an answer to. As you breathe in, ask the question. As you breathe out, listen for an answer. (Don't answer the question yourself.)

4. When you are making a simple choice, ask yourself, "Is this wise mind?"

THE FOUR STYLES OF MINDFULNESS

A common question about mindfulness is how it relates to meditation. Are they the same thing or unrelated? Mindfulness can be thought of as an umbrella that incorporates different types of practices. Meditation, as well as other practices like mindful movement, various spiritual practices, and loving kindness, are types of mindfulness.

Meditation is a form of mindfulness that involves a length of time set aside to sit quietly and focus on a particular thing. While this type of meditation isn't part of the skills modules of DBT, we can look at some meditative traditions and see links to the types of mindfulness exercises we use in DBT.

In the Buddhist tradition that Linehan learned from while developing DBT, there are four types of meditation that we can see in our mindfulness skills. These are known as concentrative mindfulness, generative mindfulness, receptive mindfulness, and reflective mindfulness.

Concentrative Mindfulness

In concentrative practices, we focus all our attention on one thing. In traditional meditation, that one thing might be the breath. This can be uncomfortable for new students, people who deal with anxiety or big emotions, or those who have a history of trauma. Fortunately, the breath is not the only option as a focus point. Anything we can focus on with any of our five senses (sight, sound, touch, taste, and hearing) or our internal sense (like our breath, muscles, or other body sensations) can be the thing we concentrate our attention on. Later, as we get more skillful, we might focus on other internal experiences, like thoughts or feelings.

When we are concentrating on the one thing, we will inevitably get distracted. This is the natural condition of the human mind and doesn't mean we've failed. When this happens, we can just notice the distraction, not judge it, and then return our concentration to the one thing—over and over and over again. It's important not to judge ourselves for being "bad at mindfulness." Like any other muscle, it will not be strong or disciplined in the beginning. It is and will always be a process.

CONCENTRATION MEDITATION

Set aside 5 to 10 minutes each day and choose one thing to focus on. Perhaps one day it could be an object that you can see and touch. Another day it could be a single item of food—notice its smell, texture, and flavor as you eat it. Yet another day you might try just observing your inhale and exhale, following the entire sequence of a breath and counting to 10 breaths before starting over again at one. If you find that focusing on your breath produces anxiety, choose a body part, like your left foot, and notice all the parts of your foot, one at a time.

Write down your experiences in your notebook.

Generative Mindfulness

The goal of generative mindfulness practices is to purposefully generate positive emotions. One of the most well-known types of generative practice is known as loving kindness, in which we work to generate kind feelings or compassion for the self and others, simply beginning by thinking of a person and thinking kind thoughts about them. We aim to extend this loving kindness toward not only people we value but also those we struggle with. Sometimes it is most difficult to find this compassion toward ourselves, but compassion for self and others are tied together. Here are some suggestions for how you can practice this meditation.

LOVING KINDNESS MEDITATION

There are many loving kindness meditation recordings available on YouTube or any of the mindfulness apps. Consider trying some out until you find one you like. As a simple beginning, though, find a comfortable place to sit and settle in. After taking a few settling breaths, think of a person you love. As you think of them with warm feelings, repeat these phrases to yourself slowly, perhaps a few times: "May they be safe, may they feel loved, may they be at peace." After this, you will move on to a neutral person, then one you struggle with, and then to yourself. You can start with yourself if you are able to access kind feelings toward yourself. It can sometimes be challenging to extend these feelings toward yourself or someone you don't like. Be patient with yourself and keep practicing. It will come.

Receptive Mindfulness

Receptive mindfulness is about noticing and accepting whatever shows up in the moment. Traditionally, one would sit with eyes open while noticing all sensations and experiences that come up in the moment. This would include breath, all five senses, other bodily sensations, thoughts, emotions, and anything happening externally in the environment. Even as thoughts or judgments come up, the goal is to just observe them as they come and go. In this form of mindfulness, you are simply noticing all that is happening within and around you and observing without attaching to any of it.

RECEPTIVE MINDFULNESS MEDITATION

This type of practice can be quite challenging. A good way to try it is to find a place to sit in public where there is lots of activity happening. Sit, for instance, on a park bench for 20 minutes, staring straight ahead and just noticing what passes in front of your eyes. If you notice that you are having assessing or judging thoughts, or you are beginning to mentally describe what you're seeing, just observe these thoughts or urges and keep watching whatever passes in front of you.

Record your observations about the experience of trying to observe after the fact in your notebook.

Reflective Mindfulness

Reflective mindfulness is perhaps the most challenging practice for people who are just learning mindfulness or who have big, overwhelming emotions or difficult histories. In reflective mindfulness, the aim is to choose a particular idea or topic, perhaps some specific worry thought. While selecting a theme, the person is just open to whatever sensations, thoughts, and emotions might come up connected to the theme. This is an advanced practice because it takes time to learn or believe with confidence that the painful feelings that might come up are temporary. A person with a difficult or traumatic history could easily get pulled into reflecting deeply on how hard their life has been, and that is not likely to be beneficial.

REFLECTION MEDITATION

If you'd like to try this practice, I'd recommend setting a timer for just a few minutes. Also, choose a topic or theme that is not too terribly heavy or difficult and allow yourself to focus on what comes up around that theme. If you find yourself getting too distressed or distracted, bring your focus back to the present moment. With this and all meditation exercises, remember to be kind and patient with yourself.

Reflect on what came up during the meditation in your journal.

KEY TAKEAWAYS ....

Mindfulness can be a rather abstract concept. In this chapter, we have talked about states of mind, including emotional, rational, and wise-minded states. We've also talked about four different kinds of mindfulness exercises, which each have different functions and goals. In the next two chapters, we will get into some practical applications and talk about particular benefits of mindfulness, and then you will begin to see how to actually *do* mindfulness. The more you practice, the more it will make sense.

Key points from this chapter:
- Mindfulness is a practice and takes time to learn.
- Emotions and reason are both important but can each be unbalanced without the other.
- There are a variety of ways to practice mindfulness.
- Be patient with yourself as you learn to access your wise mind.

How to Practice DBT-Based Mindfulness

To truly live, you must have your senses open.

Mindfulness skills are designed to help us stay present in the moment without judging and rejecting our experience or, conversely, attaching to it. Another way of saying this is that sometimes in a difficult moment we want to change what's happening to make it tolerable, judge ourselves for feeling the way we do, or jump on the train with the moment's thoughts or feelings and get pulled in. Not every moment needs to be a mindful one, but in the moments when we are trying to be present, the goal is just to notice rather than change or perpetuate the moment.

"WHAT" SKILLS

When we are learning to exercise our mindfulness muscles, there are two sets of skills that we use: the "what" skills and the "how" skills. The first are the "what" skills, or *what* we do when we are being mindful. There are three "what" skills: observe, describe, and participate.

The "what" skills are each distinct activities from one another. They are meant to be done separately, one at a time. Each of the skills—observe, describe, and participate—has a different focus.

Observe

Observing is focusing on what you can experience with your five senses, or with your inner sense—called *interoception*—which is how your body communicates with your brain. These senses can be either inside or outside of your body. You can observe the feeling of your breath in your nostrils, the sensation of hunger, the color of the walls, or the feeling of running your hand along something smooth. You can also observe brain functions like thoughts or emotions. Observing is not thinking about how you would describe something. It is simply noticing or opening your awareness to sensations and experiences.

When we observe, we also do so without attachment to the moment. If observing a thought, emotion, or sensation, we are trying to step back from it and notice its natural rhythms rather than jumping on board and getting lost in it. We are simply observing a phenomenon or process, as you might observe a chemical reaction in a lab.

So often we go through life without really noticing what's happening around us. Our figurative eyes are closed, and a lot of times we think it's easier that way. Observing helps us see the present moment, the factual moment, not the moment we wish we were in. Observing helps us stay in the present reality and fully live.

OBSERVING AN OBJECT

Choose an item in your immediate environment. Notice its shape, color, size, sheen, and whether it casts a shadow. Pick it up and notice the texture and weight of it. *Only* observe physical characteristics. If you notice yourself judging the item, attaching meaning to it, or starting to describe it, simply notice your distraction. Don't judge yourself for that; just return your focus to what you can notice with your senses.

Practice observing other objects: a leaf, a rock, a candle flame. Once you've observed multiple objects, you can try observing other sensations/experiences such as touch, smell, taste, muscle tension, hunger, breathing, and the way your feet hit the ground as you walk. Then you can even move on to observing your thoughts and feelings. Just notice.

Describe

Once you have observed, you can describe. It's our natural tendency to add words to what we have noticed or observed. When mindfully describing, we are putting words to things we can experience ourselves. Note that you cannot observe what another person is feeling, thinking, or experiencing, even if you think you know based on their facial expression, words, or actions. You cannot observe something internal to another person.

Describing helps us differentiate between what we are truly sensing (seeing, hearing, touching, smelling, tasting, feeling, or thinking) and our thoughts about or interpretations of what we're sensing. Much of our emotional discomfort around events comes from these interpretations rather than the events themselves. Describing helps us tease out the difference. For example, "My child is wearing mismatched clothing" is far more neutral than "If my child goes to school like that, they might get bullied and people might think I'm a bad parent." Describing the situation—"My child is wearing clothing that doesn't match and I'm noticing that I have some worries about that"—can help us clarify what we're really responding to.

JUST THE FACTS

When describing mindfully, describe only the facts. Do not add interpretations, opinions, or judgments. You might have the experience of thinking another person doesn't like you. In reality, you can only observe the person's actions, facial expressions, or body language. Think of a time when you have seen a person acting in a way that you perceived as angry. Describe what you *actually* saw: for instance, shoulders up, fists clenched, brows drawn together, jaw clenched, or voice loud.

Actions/behaviors that I perceived as anger:

....

....

....

Participate

Participating is fully throwing yourself into life. It's doing something with all your attention on that one thing, right now, without worrying about what others are thinking. It's about being in the present moment without fixating on what happened in the past or worrying about what might happen in the future. Participating is setting your cell phone down at dinner and focusing your attention on the meal and the person you are sharing it with. It's going with the flow, being spontaneous, and doing what is needed in the moment from a wise-minded perspective. Participating is being completely immersed in whatever you're doing.

When we seek to be mindful, participation is ultimately our goal. It is the opposite of being fearful, self-conscious, distracted, reactive, excluded, or avoidant. It means not operating on autopilot or sleepwalking through life. Participation connects us with life and with other people. Participation is living fully.

THROW YOURSELF IN

Here are some ideas for practicing participation. Choose an activity that captures your attention and that you can fully throw yourself into. Write some of your own ideas to the lines on page 37 for practicing participation. Do at least one thing per day and record your experiences in your notebook.

▸ Turn up the music and dance.
▸ Sing along with music.
▸ Sing in the shower.
▸ Keep a balloon from hitting the ground.
▸ Jump rope or skip.
▸ Eat dessert and focus on it fully.

More ways I can practice participation:

....

....

....

....

....

"HOW" SKILLS

You've learned what to do when practicing mindfulness. Now we'll discuss *how* to do the "what" skills. These "how" skills set the tone of our attitudes and mind-set as we practice mindfulness and try to be present in the moment.

I mentioned earlier that the "what" skills are meant to be done separately from one another. The "how" skills, in contrast, are qualities that can and should be incorporated together into our practice of the "what" skills. We aim to behave nonjudgmentally, one-mindfully, and effectively all at the same time.

Nonjudgmentally

Judgments are part of life. Sometimes we judge to determine the difference or our preference between two things. In some contexts, we need to judge to help us make decisions, like judging whether food is safe to eat or whether something is legal. When we are dealing with emotions, though, judgments can add confusion and even suffering. When we are being mindful, we want to deal with only the facts, so judgments or evaluations—especially ones based in unrealistic expectations or that lead to lack of compassion for ourselves or others—need to be set aside. Judgments that help us be aware of consequences, such as whether something is objectively safe or will get us in trouble, are okay.

Because judgments can be hard on our emotions and relationships, we recognize that they often aren't helpful. It's more effective to solve a problem than to focus on whether something *should* be the way it is. When we focus on judgments, we can easily get stuck in the emotions rather than seeing the situation clearly and thus being able to determine a solution.

To be clear, the goal of nonjudgment isn't to approve of things we disapprove of or to keep our preferences, values, or opinions to ourselves. The goal is to be aware of judgments and to set them aside when they get in the way of accepting the actual moment we are in.

MISSING PERSONS REPORT

Think of a person you know or a famous person. Write down a description of the person as though you're filling out a missing persons report. Only describe the factual aspects of their physical appearance: for example, height, weight, build, hair/ eye/skin color, and clothing. Avoid things like pretty, ugly, cool, athletic, artsy, or stylish. All of those things are judgments. Notice the moments when you are quick to judge and try to find the objective description instead. How does it feel to make the choice not to judge?

Description of a person:

One-Mindfully

Doing something *one-mindfully* means doing only one thing at a time. It's the opposite of multitasking. When practicing mindfulness, the goal is to be fully present in the moment that's happening and only that moment. Whatever you're focused on, whether a task or thought or emotion, try to do just that one thing. If you notice that your thoughts are wandering or there's an urge to do multiple things at once or let your mind wander, just observe that urge and bring your focus back to the one thing and the one moment.

One-mindfulness isn't just about tasks; it ultimately helps us manage our emotions because we can choose the one thing we are focusing on, rather than being tossed about by our thoughts or emotions, or feeling they'll last forever. The importance of this can't be overstated: Knowing that a difficult moment is not permanent helps you survive that difficult moment. Being able to remember that even triggered memories are just that and the past is over, as well as knowing the future is not here yet, means that even a difficult moment can be tolerated.

Note: Some tasks are complex, with multiple aspects involved. You can still do them one-mindfully—one step at a time.

JUST ONE THING

Choose one thing to do, and do only that thing. If there are multiple steps to what you're doing, do just one step at a time and try not to let your mind wander to the next step. Any time your thoughts wander, simply notice that they're wandering and return to the one thing. After you've finished, record your observations in your notebook. Here are a few ideas. Feel free to add some of your own.

▸ Wash dishes by hand. Focus on each sensation of moving the sponge or cloth around the dish. Notice the soap bubbles and the temperature and feeling of the water.

▸ Make tea or coffee and focus on each step of the process.

▸ Eat a meal without doing anything else. Focus your attention completely on the experience.

▸ Go for a walk and focus all your attention on the experience of walking.

Effectively

Doing something *effectively* means doing what works. It's knowing what your goal is in any given situation and then doing what is needed to achieve it. Sometimes this means playing by the rules rather than digging in your heels and insisting that you're right. Your goal is to find solutions and make things work in the context you've found yourself in rather than thinking about what you wish were happening. When you're trying to be effective, it helps to be open to trying new ways to problem-solve, finding different solutions, and learning from your mistakes.

DO WHAT WORKS

Think of a time when you felt like digging in your heels or insisting that you were right. Think about what that felt like. Did insisting you were right help you get your goal in the situation, or did it get in the way? Is there something you could have shifted to accomplish your goal? Write down your observations in your journal or in the space provided.

Situation:

....

....

....

....

Your "right" view:

....

....

....

....

What you might have done to be more effective:

_____

_____

_____

KEY TAKEAWAYS ....

The scientific mindfulness that we teach in DBT can help us increase focus, reduce suffering, and be more present in our lives. It can also help us have some freedom from feeling controlled by our thoughts and feelings. We begin to develop our mindfulness muscles through practicing the "what" skills—observe, describe, and participate—and the "how" skills—nonjudgmentally, one-mindfully, and effectively. You start with simple things like observing or describing objects, and as you gain some skills for managing your emotions and thoughts, you can turn your mindfulness skills into deeper things, like mindfulness of current thoughts or emotions.

Key points from this chapter:

▸ You can't "do it wrong" in mindfulness, so be patient as you learn.

▸ Try to stay only in the moment.

▸ Do one thing at a time.

▸ Don't judge your judging.

Incorporating Mindfulness into Your Routine

Mindfulness is just an idea unless you put it into practice. What you feed grows.

Some people come to DBT with hesitancy or even suspicion of mindfulness. Others think it's just woo-woo nonsense. There's lots of misinformation out there on what mindfulness is, and some of the forms of practice might not be for you. However, the scientific form of mindfulness that we teach in DBT is helpful for anyone who can benefit from being able to focus on one thing. Whether a task, an object, or a sensation, we all find ourselves in a position of needing to focus on something. When we commonly experience feeling overwhelmed by thoughts or feelings, it can be freeing to be able to choose what we're going to focus on. There isn't room here for a deep dive into all the ways to be mindful or the many types of exercises, but hopefully these chapters will start you thinking about how to establish your own mindfulness practice.

ESTABLISHING A MINDFULNESS PRACTICE

This week, you will learn about setting yourself up for success in establishing a mindfulness practice, including making space (both physically and mentally) and creating a routine. Some of the most basic things to know have to do with how to sit when practicing. For most exercises, you will start by sitting in a well-supported position, with your spine upright and feet flat on the floor. Some may choose to sit cross-legged on a meditation cushion or pillow. For some activities, you might even lie down flat or stand. If these positions are not accessible, try to find a posture that allows you to not be distracted by the position you are in. Next, either close your eyes or cast your eyes without focusing on a spot some distance in front of you. These basic tips will reduce distractions and help you focus on the task instead of what's happening around you.

Note: Many exercises assume certain physical and cognitive capabilities. If there are reasons that you cannot follow the directions exactly as written, you can still participate. Make whatever adaptations you need to make without judgment. If you have a mind, you can be mindful. Don't let differences in your body or in the way you learn stop you.

As mentioned earlier in the book, Linehan included mindfulness rather than meditation in the DBT skills because traditional meditation, which is often focused on observing the breath, can be dysregulating for many of our clients. Focusing on breath can actually make it hard to breathe for some folks. This is just one example of adaptations that we can make to the way we learn mindfulness. Everyone learns differently, and people who might be considered neurodiverse in some way might not relate to the traditional way mindfulness is taught. It is important to note that this is where the core functions of observing and non-judgment come in. As you begin to learn, observe the parts of mindfulness that you connect with and those you don't. Don't judge yourself for the challenges; simply notice them. Then you can adapt. There is no one adaptation that will work for everyone. The mindfulness world is only recently catching up and learning to teach in a way that is accessible for all learning styles and for folks with a trauma history.

Making Space

When we hear about people meditating or praying, we might envision a serene space with no distractions. A photo-ready, beautiful environment can absolutely enhance our practice of meditation or mindfulness, but it is not necessary. In meditation and mindfulness, we are trying to be present with whatever moment we find ourselves in. The space doesn't have to be distraction-free, though it can be. What does seem to be very helpful is to have a purposeful, dedicated plan for your practice. My very first mindfulness trainer, Randy Wolbert, told my group of trainees that he had a spot halfway between his bathroom and his kitchen where he stopped for a few minutes of mindfulness practice every morning before drinking his coffee. Perhaps you have a space and time like that where you'll be uninterrupted, and perhaps you don't. You can still set apart a time and space to begin to practice.

CREATING PHYSICAL SPACE

Where and how would you like to set aside time for a dedicated practice? I'd encourage you to start with five minutes a day, several days a week, in a place where you can sit as comfortably and uninterrupted as possible. When I first started, I would keep my eyes closed after waking up in the morning and just take a few minutes in bed to focus on my breathing. Now, once my kids are on the school bus, I clear off their breakfast from the table so that I have a sliver of calm space and try to mindfully eat my breakfast and drink my tea. What might work for you? You can be creative about the where and how. Just try to be consistent. Jot down some possibilities here or in your notebook:

FINDING MENTAL SPACE

What does it mean to create mental space? In learning mindfulness, one of the benefits we receive is the ability to see that there is space between the breaths, between steps, between sounds, between thoughts, and, perhaps most important, between stimulus and action. It can feel like our thoughts, emotions, and urges are relentless, but we can learn to find the pause in between. We can also learn to find the space between our urges and our actions, which means we have a choice about our responses and reactions. This exercise encourages you to look for the pause or space between your thoughts.

Settle into a mindful posture, with eyes closed or cast at a fixed spot in front of you. Take a couple of breaths, turning your attention to the present moment. Next, begin to notice your thoughts and label their categories: planning thoughts, worry thoughts, thoughts about the past, thoughts about the future, judgment thoughts, etc. Imagine you're watching a gently flowing river. Small boats go by, one at a time. On each boat, place a category of thought that you labeled. Watch those thought boats go by, floating down the river. Notice what it's like to observe your thoughts instead of jumping on the boats. Now look for the space between the boats or thoughts and see if you can increase the space between them.

Setting a Routine

In DBT groups as well as therapist meetings, trainings, or other gatherings, we always begin with a mindfulness exercise. We do this to encourage us all to keep mindfulness at the forefront of what we are doing and to learn about different ways to practice, but it has another benefit: slowing down our minds so that we can focus on the discussions to come. By starting our meetings with a brief mindfulness exercise, we bring our focus into the present, setting aside all the rest just for the moment.

The goal of setting up your own routine is to make sure you have a regular opportunity to focus on your purpose, as well as giving your mindfulness muscles a regular workout. Several things can help you be more successful at forming this new habit. We've already discussed making physical and mental space. Here are some more things to consider.

SETTING UP YOUR PRACTICE

Go ahead and open up your notebook and write down at least one option for each of the following questions:

1. Where can I practice?

2. When can I practice?

3. After trying each "what" skill, which type came easiest? (To start with, focus on the kind of mindfulness that feels most accessible to you.)

4. What gets in the way of me trying? (Distractions? Emotions? Judging myself for not being able to focus?)

5. What are some ways I might overcome these obstacles?

6. How can I make a commitment to this practice? (Adding it to the calendar on my phone? Setting a reminder alert? Staying accountable with a friend or family member?)

   Additional reminders:
   ▸ It's a learning process.
   ▸ When you get distracted, just notice and return your focus to the one thing.
   ▸ Try not to judge yourself for getting distracted.
   ▸ When you judge yourself, don't judge your judging. Just notice and refocus.

IMPROVING YOUR DAY-TO-DAY LIFE WITH MINDFULNESS

In DBT, we focus on scientific mindfulness to help us:
▸ Reduce suffering and increase happiness.
▸ Increase control of the mind.
▸ Experience reality as it is.

In the broader research on mindfulness, the practice has been linked to a variety of benefits, including increased focus; decreased rumination or obsessive thoughts, worry, stress, anxiety, and emotional reactivity; increased relationship satisfaction; and even improvement in various health conditions like diabetes and high blood pressure. We will explore several of these benefits in this section.

Closer to home, mindfulness can help us have some control over our thoughts and emotions rather than feeling like we're on a roller coaster or in an out-of-control car that our thoughts, feelings, and circumstances are driving.

Experiencing Great Focus

Following in the footsteps of multiple studies before it, a research study at the University of California, Santa Barbara, explored whether participation in a mindfulness course could improve students' performance on standardized tests. The study specifically looked at improving reading comprehension and working memory as well as decreasing distraction. The results indicated that practicing mindfulness had a positive impact on reading comprehension and working memory, which, in turn, decreased distraction. In other words, staying engaged in a task decreased distraction, and the participants were better able to stay focused on the task after practicing mindfulness. This is just one study, but there are many that have shown similar results.

Mindfulness engages our brain in such a way that we continue to increase our ability to choose where we will focus our thoughts. We get there by forming new pathways in our brains rather than defaulting to our old, rutted thought roads.

FOCUS ON THE BREATH

Choose one thing to focus on and return your thoughts to it again and again and again. For this exercise, we will focus on our breath. Find your preferred mindfulness posture and notice the cycle of your breath. Follow it from the beginning of a full inhale, through the pause, and all the way through the entire exhale. Keep following your breath. If you get distracted, just notice that you got distracted, without judgment, and return your focus to your breath as many times as you need. You might try this for five minutes just before working on a job or school task. Record your experience in your notebook.

If this is too uncomfortable or anxiety-inducing here at the beginning of learning mindfulness, you could focus on your belly, rib cage, or shoulders instead, noticing how they shift as you breathe normally.

Experiencing Deeper Relaxation

People often think that if they aren't feeling relaxed by the end of a mindfulness exercise, they must have done it wrong. They haven't. Relaxation is not, in fact, the goal of mindfulness. However, relaxation is invariably one of the long-term benefits of having a mindfulness practice. This is due, in part, to the fact that many mindfulness exercises stimulate the parasympathetic, or calming, part of our nervous system. It is also true that when we feel less out of control (of thoughts, emotions, stress, etc.), we are able to relax better.

BODY SCAN AND PROGRESSIVE MUSCLE RELAXATION

Body scans and progressive muscle relaxation are great ways to promote relaxation. Either sitting in your mindfulness posture or lying down, you will start at either your head or toes and work your way to the other end. Start by taking several full breaths and exhaling completely. For a body scan, you will simply turn your attention to each body part, one after the other: feet, calves, thighs, seat, lower back, upper back and shoulders, belly, chest, fists, forearms, biceps, neck, head, and face. Simply pay attention to any sensations you notice in each group while continuing to breathe deeply. You can add to this exercise by doing progressive muscle relaxation, carefully tensing each muscle group on your inhale and gently releasing on your exhale, then moving on to the next muscle group. Record your experience in your notebook. There are many guided versions of these exercises available online. Finding one you like and repeating it a few times is a great way to learn this technique.

Creating a Healthy Mind-Body Connection

People have long debated the relationship between mind and body. The philosophical questions are beyond the focus of this workbook, but the link is not. We have known for a long time that the mind can communicate to the body. You think of an upcoming meeting or test and feel nervous; your heart beats a little faster and you get jittery. The mind is telling the body that there's cause for anxiety. However, we also know that there are even more nerve pathways that go from the body to the brain (80 percent) than from the brain to the body (20 percent). Our body can tell our brain that we are hungry or hot or cold. Likewise, we can also use breathing, grounding, or relaxation exercises to tell the brain we are safe and it's okay not to panic.

FIVE SENSES EXERCISE

Grounding is a great way to send a calming message to the brain when you're feeling concerned or stressed by bringing your awareness to the space and time that you are currently in. There are many ways to ground. Practicing these techniques when you're calm will make them more accessible when you're not. Try this 5-4-3-2-1 exercise to get started. Identify the following things and write them down in your notebook. You can do this exercise mentally and on-the-go whenever you're feeling anxious or need help grounding in the present moment.

- ▶ Five things you can see.
- ▶ Four things you can touch.
- ▶ Three things you can hear.
- ▶ Two things you can smell.
- ▶ One thing you can taste.

Calming Your Emotions

I would never tell you that mindfulness can magically fix your emotional suffering overnight. However, it can help. As we'll learn in weeks 7 to 9, emotions have important functions in our lives. They communicate important things to us and to others. They can also be overwhelming, and our tendency when this happens is to want to shut them down. We know, though, that avoiding or suppressing emotions ultimately makes them worse. To manage our emotions, we must first acknowledge and identify them. The trick then is to not get attached to them, to not jump on the emotional train that will end up making us feel worse. Mindfulness allows us to observe with a tiny bit of distance, to be present without letting the emotions drive the car, so to speak. This can be quite a challenging skill to learn, but with practice it will come.

NOTICING YOUR EMOTIONS

This skill will be far more manageable and accessible in difficult moments if you practice it first in the less fueled ones. Grab your notebook and write down an emotion that you're experiencing. Start with one that you can identify feeling but that isn't too big or overwhelming. Once you've identified it, give it a rating from 0 to 100, with 100 being the most intensely you've ever felt it. Write it down. Next, say to yourself, "I'm noticing that I'm feeling _____" (sad, happy, anxious, confused, frustrated, etc.).

So instead of identifying with the feeling by saying "I'm so mad!" say instead something like "Oh, look! There's anger," "I'm noticing that I'm feeling disappointed," or "Hello, anxiety." After you've practiced this for a while, notice whether your rating of the emotion comes down after reframing it. You'll be surprised what a difference that little bit of distance can do for you.

KEY TAKEAWAYS . . . .

Mindfulness is an ancient practice with many applications and benefits. You're only getting an overview here, but it's a good place to start. Our goal is not to live in a constant state of mindfulness but rather to have access to it at any moment.

By setting aside time and space to practice, we are more likely to be able to establish the new habit of practicing mindfulness. While the goal is to be able to be present in our lives, we also gain benefits such as increased relaxation, focus, connection between our minds and bodies, and even a greater sense of calm.

Key points from this chapter:
- ▸ Practice mindfulness on purpose.
- ▸ Don't judge yourself as you're learning.
- ▸ Keep trying.
- ▸ Freedom is worth the effort of learning something new.

Managing Crises with Distress Tolerance

It may feel like the night will never end,
but morning will come.

In part 1, we looked at dialectics, or the balancing of opposites. We identified that the main dialectic in DBT is acceptance and change. Not only is this the balance of approaches taken by a DBT therapist, but also it is the balance of the types of skills we need to learn as we seek to both accept our realities, including tolerating our difficulties, and to change the things we can. Mindfulness and distress tolerance are focused on acceptance of our current reality, while the emotion regulation and inter-personal effectiveness skills we will learn in the second half of the book are focused on change and problem-solving.

To tolerate distress is to get through these difficult moments without making them worse, or to get through a night of over-whelming emotions and urges without adding problematic coping methods to the mix. Over the next three weeks, we will be focused on skills to help us survive crises and accept things we aren't able to change—or aren't able to change yet.

WHAT IS DISTRESS TOLERANCE?

Everyone experiences stress, such as situations that make us nervous or require extra energy reserves to cope with. Deadlines, conflicts, life changes . . . all these things can be stressful. Things can be a little stressful or a lot stressful, but generally we can figure out a way to get through them.

Distress is different from stress. Distress is a state of being that happens when our emotional state overloads the rational part of our brain, called the prefrontal cortex. Like a fulcrum, the emotional part of our brain and logical part balance each other. At any given moment, one or the other is more active, but they usually keep each other in check. There are moments, though, when the emotional brain gets so activated that it overloads the logical part. In these moments, we cannot think our way out of distress. We have to bring down the emotion or reset our nervous system to get it to come down.

A QUICK TIP

The TIP skills are designed to be used when emotional arousal is extremely high and the nervous system is overloaded or on high alert. They're for when your emotions are so intense that you can't really process information or figure out what else to do. The acronym *TIP* stands for temperature, intense exercise, and paced breathing and paired muscle relaxation. These techniques all stimulate the parasympathetic, or calming, part of your nervous system, and help bring activation down quickly.

Temperature

The *T* in TIP stands for *temperature*. This skill is one of the first that we teach clients in DBT because it is so easily accessible and works so quickly. Changing the body's temperature can quickly decrease the intensity of an emotion. Holding your breath and placing your face in ice water for 30 seconds can bring your heart rate down from exercise target range to resting range almost immediately. This happens because it triggers what is called the *dive response*, which is an involuntary physiological reset of the nervous system.

Note: Keep water above 50°F. If you have heart issues or a history of eating disorders, please consult with your doctor before trying this technique. Some adaptations are offered in the following exercises.

Intense Exercise

The *I* in TIP stands for *intense exercise*. If you are feeling overwhelmed emotionally and can't get yourself to settle, going for a run or engaging in some other exercise can be extremely helpful. Again, the goal is to get your heart rate into target range, knowing that it will then naturally come down once the exertion is finished.

If you have physical limitations that prevent you from this kind of movement, or if it is inadvisable or not possible for you to get your heart into cardio range, you can still find ways to move or change your line of sight. A change of scenery, fresh air, a view of the outside, and any movement of your limbs or body can go a long way to letting your brain know you're not stuck and it's okay to turn off the alarm bells of your nervous system. Feeling physically stuck can absolutely feed our panic; any movement and breathing at all can help counteract it.

Paced Breathing

There is only one *P* in TIP, but there are two skills included. The first *P* in TIP stands for *paced breathing*. There are many breathing exercises out there that can work similarly, including square breathing, 4-7-8 breathing, and various forms of breathing found in yoga. A good place to start is to begin to slow your breathing down. Inhale for four counts and exhale for six. It is important for your exhale to be longer than your inhale by at least a couple of counts. This is because your exhale stimulates the calming part of your nervous system. The more you practice paced breathing, the easier it will be to use anytime or anywhere. It is a great skill to use in public settings because you can do it without anyone noticing.

Paired Muscle Relaxation

The second *P* in TIP stands for *paired muscle relaxation*. This is another technique that you can find recordings of online and in mindfulness apps. You can also do it on your own. Find a comfortable place to sit or lie down, and start either at your head or toes. One pair of body parts at a time, tense the muscles for a few seconds and then quickly release them, moving on to the next muscle group. Other than being cautious of any muscle issues, this is an extremely effective way to relax your body, which in turn sends the message to your brain that it is safe to settle.

COLD-WATER PLUNGE

Fill a bowl or sink with ice water, hold your breath, and plunge your face into the water for 30 seconds. Take a breath at 15 seconds if necessary. Check your heart rate before and after. How do you feel?

If you're unable to do this full version of cold-water TIP, you can try another variation. Splash cold water on your face or wrists, hold an ice cube, drink something very cold, hold an ice pack on your face, take a cold shower, or jump in a cold lake or pool. These alternatives may not work quite as quickly, but they can still help settle your system down.

BUYING YOURSELF SOME SPACE AND TIME WITH STOP

Linehan points out all through DBT that our emotions come with action urges. When we're afraid, we want to run. When we're angry, we want to attack. When we love, we want to embrace. Sometimes it makes sense to act on these urges, such as in a situation where there is an imminent danger; in that case, it makes sense to run or to avoid the source of our fear. However, when we are dealing with distress or overwhelming emotions, our action urges are often impulsive urges that will get us in trouble or make the situation worse. Learning to slow down and respond wisely, rather than react, can help us deal only with the trouble we already have and not add more consequences from impulsive attempts to escape or avoid our discomfort. It can also mean less hits to our self-respect. If we can slow ourselves down and act out of wise mind, we can buy ourselves some time and stay in control.

Linehan recognized the effectiveness of buying that time and developed the STOP skill as one of the first things we can do to interrupt the momentum of crisis.

Stop

When you feel like you're about to get out of control, stop yourself. Freeze in place. Physically stop yourself in your tracks, and don't move a muscle.

Remember in chapter 1 when we discussed the importance of mental practice in building a new habit (page 16)? You can combine mental practice with a physical component in this skill to help your brain make a new connection: that the act of freezing prevents you from following the strong impulse to act in a destructive way. The new connection you're making is that there is another option besides the old, habitual behaviors. In this case, the new option is that you can use these techniques to buy you some time before you act.

Take a Step Back

Take a big step backward. While initially learning the skill, do this physically if you're able to. Later, it can be a mental step back. You are interrupting any momentum you might be building toward that impulsive action and telling your brain to do the opposite, or at least to slow down. This gives you literal or figurative space from the situation and gives you time to think. Breathe deeply until the urge starts to fade or your intense emotions start to come down.

Observe

Observe what is happening around you and inside you. Notice thoughts, emotions, and body sensations. Notice how other people are acting or responding and how they're involved in what you're experiencing. Gather the facts and figure out what you can do in the situation. Use mindfulness to gather information without judgment. Mindfulness is not a separate skill from all the others; it's the foundation. Observing brings the intentionality and focus of mindfulness into the moment of crisis and allows us to get some clarity on what is really happening instead of being swept away in our urges and emotions.

Proceed Mindfully

Act intentionally. Figure out what your goal is and do what is needed to do to move toward it. Ask yourself what will make things better long term, not just what will feel better right now. If you have a particular behavior that often gets you in trouble, use the same body part to do something different. For example, if your mouth gets you in trouble by yelling, use your tongue to count your teeth. Actions like this may sound silly, but these practices are powerful ways to interrupt habitual behaviors and create new possibilities.

These techniques not only buy you more time but also communicate new ways of functioning to your brain. As stated before, the physical component helps cement those new connections. Once you are practiced at the skill, it will become an internalized process.

STOP EXERCISE

S: Think of a situation that usually results in impulsive behavior for you and imagine it happening in this moment. Think about the emotion it brings up, and identify the impulsive action urge. March in place, and as you start to feel the emotion and urge, freeze in place. Keep thinking about how upset you are but stay frozen, not moving a muscle.

T: As you feel the urge to yell or run, take a physical step back. Give yourself some space from the situation.

O: Look around. Notice what is happening around you. Is the situation still happening? What's happening inside your body? Are your thoughts racing? Heart rate and breathing sped up? Fists clenched? Try to observe the facts and not jump to conclusions.

P: Based on what you've observed, think about what is possible in the moment. Can this problem be solved right now? Or is it better to wait? Can you do something to help you tolerate it? Would it be better to walk away, get some sleep, and come back to it in the morning? How can you take care of yourself right now so that you won't feel bad for impulsive behavior later?

Write down your experiences for each letter in your notebook. You can do this for several different scenarios, thinking through difficult situations where you've acted impulsively in the past. The goal is not to make you feel bad for the past; it's to help you identify more effective ways to cope in the future.

KEEP STOPPING

Practice the STOP skill at least three times this week when you are experiencing heightened emotions. Practicing in situations that aren't quite crisis-level will more likely make the skill come to mind when you *are* in crisis. See the following example, then use the blank chart to fill in your own.

SITUATION	EMOTION OR URGE	WHAT YOU OBSERVED	HOW YOU PROCEEDED
Customer at work talking down to me	Anger, shame, wanting to hide or lash out	They're talking over me, demanding I help, and asking for my manager; I have a red face; I'm tense in the shoulders but not in the stomach; urge to run; my manager is supporting me	Making sure my manager is stepping in, asking for a break, going back to break room and breathing, splashing water on my face, settling before going back to work

SITUATION	EMOTION OR URGE	WHAT YOU OBSERVED	HOW YOU PROCEEDED

USING DOUBLE PROS AND CONS

Making a pros-and-cons list is often a helpful way to make a decision. It is even more helpful to make what we call a *double pros-and-cons list*. To do this, you will list the pros and cons of acting on an urge, and then you will list the pros and cons of *not* acting on it. It may seem like it would be repetitive, but you'll be surprised at what comes up and how significant the subtle differences can be.

Let's look at an example. Say your habit when you get overwhelmed is to drink until you stop feeling stressed. A double pros-and-cons list might look like this:

	PROS	CONS
Acting On the Urge (Urge: Drinking)	Feel better quickly Feel good briefly Not have to think about stress Not have to solve the problem Not have to feel	Problem still not solved Cost Hangover Shame/guilt* Relapse Support system worried, disappointed
Not Acting On the Urge	No guilt No money spent Support system not worried Can deal with the problem Learning not to avoid Can use other skills Feel good about myself No hangover or relapse	Have to stay with the emotions Can't avoid It's hard to do Not a quick solution

DOUBLE PROS-AND-CONS EXERCISE

This is a skill that is often not accessible in the midst of a crisis. I suggest sitting down and making a list when you are not in crisis and keeping it on hand so that you can look at it to remind yourself of your clear thinking when you do get into a crisis. Reminding yourself of times when you've been skillful or thought clearly and with confidence can be key in acting skillfully when in crisis. It can also help you remember that this moment is not permanent.

Identify a repeated problematic behavior that you are trying to change and fill out the list. Once you've made your list, go back and star (*), circle, or highlight the things on the list that seem to carry more impact than others. It may not be the category with the most things listed that wins; identify the key factors for you that seem most important to help you make your decision.

	PROS	CONS
Acting On the Urge **(Urge: _____)**		
Not Acting On the Urge		

EVERYDAY DOUBLE PROS AND CONS

Double pros and cons can also be used for everyday decisions. Feel free to use the chart for a noncrisis decision you're trying to make.

	PROS	CONS
Acting On the Urge/Making the Decision **(Urge/Decision: _____)**		
Not Acting On the Urge/Not Making the Decision		

KEY TAKEAWAYS ....

In this chapter, we learned about some additional crisis survival skills that can help us tolerate extremely difficult moments without making things worse. We've learned about a skill that works really quickly (TIP), a skill that buys us time (STOP), and a skill that gives us a chance to plan ahead (Pros and Cons). With these skills, we are building our options for coping with distress in ways that will build our confidence and self-respect as we become more and more skillful.

Key points from this chapter:

▸ Plan ahead with Pros and Cons.

▸ Reset your nervous system by using TIP skills to stimulate the calming part of your system.

▸ Use STOP to buy yourself some time before acting on the intense emotions.

Using Distress Tolerance to Get Through the Week without Making It Worse

Things don't have to be perfect. I can get through this if I just slow down a little and get some space from my emotions.

The skills this week continue our work in the category of crisis survival. These tools will help you get some space from the difficulty of the moment so that you don't act on destructive urges or respond in impulsive ways that can get you in trouble or make the situation worse. The IMPROVE skills (imagery, meaning, prayer, relaxation, one thing in the moment, vacation, and encouragement), for example, shift the moment enough to make it more tolerable while not taking you out of it entirely. These skills require practice. They don't come naturally when we are overwhelmed unless we have rehearsed them when we aren't in crisis. The more you practice these techniques, the more likely they will be to come to mind as options when you're in a tough moment.

WHAT WE MEAN BY "CRISIS"

A crisis is a single, time-limited experience of true distress. This happens when your thoughts or emotions get so big that they feel like they're going to overwhelm you. Perhaps something triggered a painful memory, emotions have been building all day and you're tired and can't tamp them down anymore, or you've had a conflict with someone and can't imagine that it will get better and therefore you can't believe you will survive. It might also be that several circumstances have converged to create a situation without an immediate solution, such as having unexpected bills come up when you've just spent too much money, have no food, and rent is due. Getting to the point of feeling the moment is simply intolerable and it can't immediately be solved is what we call a crisis.

Crisis survival skills are specifically designed to get us through the moment of crisis or overload without making it worse. When distressed, we often have urges to use impulsive or harmful behaviors that can make us feel better in the moment but make things worse in the long run. These skills are meant to make the moment or situation more tolerable so we may return to a regulated emotional state. However, if we use these skills too often when we really need to be solving the problem, they will become less effective. The problem that we are avoiding solving will also likely get worse while we avoid it. It's important to remember that these are tools to be used in a crisis, not merely when we are feeling uncomfortable.

CRISIS SURVIVAL SKILLS

One of our goals in DBT is to decrease behaviors that may have helped in the past but are getting in the way of our quality of life or keeping us from moving forward. These behaviors vary as much as the people working on them, but some common targets are self-harm, addictions, risky sex, overspending, binging and purging, and a variety of forms of lashing out in anger or avoiding. In order of priority, we address behaviors that are: life-threatening, interfere with being able to engage in therapy, and decrease our quality of life. Behaviors that consistently worry the people around us can also fall into the category of ineffective.

Crisis survival skills are meant to help us get through extremely difficult moments that are unavoidable without using these ineffective behaviors because while they might help us feel better in the moment, they tend to add more problems to the mix in the long run.

Distraction Skills

Distraction is useful when emotions threaten to overwhelm you, you can't solve the problem right away, or you have to be able to function despite the intensity. It can easily be overused if we use it to avoid emotions. In a crisis, though, distraction can be extremely helpful in keeping us from acting on problematic urges. It can also buy us some much-needed time when we can't solve the problems leading to our distress—or can't solve them yet. Distraction allows us to focus our attention on something besides our emotions or worries.

Distracting Yourself with Wise Mind ACCEPTS

Here are some categories of the types of activities you can use to distract yourself. A helpful way to remember these seven sets of distracting skills is the acronym ACCEPTS. By giving us some distance from the distress, distraction can help us function in a wise-minded way, even if we aren't currently feeling very wise minded. It can also sometimes shift the emotions a little bit.

Activities—getting involved in an activity that claims your attention can help take your mind off your emotions:

▸ Watch a show
▸ Listen to music
▸ Go for a walk
▸ Work out
▸ Make something

Contributions—helping someone else can take your mind off your own troubles:

▸ Do something nice for another person
▸ Volunteer or contribute to a cause
▸ Send a nice text
▸ Call a friend and ask them how they're doing

SKILL	CRISIS SITUATION	WHEN/WHAT YOU DID	TIME TRIED
Activities	*Argument with Mom*	*Watched a movie*	*2 hours*
Contributions			
Comparisons			
Emotions			
Push away			
Thoughts			
Sensations	*Worried because person I'm dating hasn't texted*	*Went for a run, then hot shower*	*1 hour*

Comparisons—helps you realize this moment isn't permanent:
▶ Compare yourself to someone who has it worse
▶ Watch shows about other people's problems
▶ Remember a time when you felt differently

Emotions—do something that triggers a different strong emotion:
▶ Watch a comedy, horror, or other emotional movie
▶ Listen to emotional music
▶ Read a book or old letters

Pushing away—push the emotions away entirely for a little while:
▶ Imagine putting the situation in a box on the shelf
▶ Leave the situation for a while, either mentally or physically
▶ Refuse to think about whatever's bothering you, saying no when thoughts come up

SKILL	EMOTION INTENSITY BEFORE/AFTER (0 TO 100)	EXPERIENCES
Activities	85/55	*Took my mind off it, made me laugh*
Contributions		
Comparisons		
Emotions		
Push away		
Thoughts		
Sensations	90/65	*Still stressed but able to go to sleep*

Thoughts—get your mind on other things for a while:

- ▸ Count to 98 backward and forward by 7
- ▸ Do a puzzle
- ▸ Recite a poem or song
- ▸ Watch or read something

Sensations—get your body involved in something else:

- ▸ Take a bath or shower
- ▸ Exercise
- ▸ Dance
- ▸ Hold ice
- ▸ Squeeze a ball or wring a towel

WISE MIND ACCEPTS SKILLS EXERCISE

Practice each of the skills at least twice. Use the table above to record your experiences in your notebook.

MAKING A DISTRACTION PLAN

Make a distraction plan for situations that are often distressing for you. Hang it up on your bathroom mirror or put it next to your bed so it's handy when a crisis arises. Planning ahead and reviewing the plan also means it's more likely to come to mind when you need it. Check out the example of a situation and plan on the next page. Then use the same format to start creating your own plan for situations that regularly come up for you.

SITUATION	EMOTIONS/URGES THAT COME UP	SKILLS TO TRY
Waiting for friend or partner to reply to texts	Fear that they're ghosting, self-criticism, urge to self-harm, urge to keep texting repeatedly with increasing demands	Ask roommate to watch a funny movie with me (activity, emotion), push away if thoughts come back up during movie, drink hot tea (sensation)

SELF-SOOTHING SKILLS

Self-soothing is another physical skill that helps with regulating the nervous system. The goal is to get the calming part of your nervous system active. Doing so will help your emotions come down as your body communicates safety and calm to your brain. Self-soothing is a type of mindfulness that brings your attention to the moment and extend kindness and compassion toward yourself.

Self-soothing can be used in the midst of distress or crisis, but it can also be used as a regular practice to reduce your vulnerability or likelihood of having big emotional responses in the future.

Soothing Yourself with the Five Senses

Self-soothing uses the five senses to help us tolerate pain and lower our vulnerability. Here are some ideas for how you can use the senses as you begin to think about what might be soothing for you.

Vision: looking at a view of something beautiful: the starry sky, someone you love, photos of pretty things or places you've visited, photos of pets or loved ones, a clean space, nature, art/performance

Hearing: music, nature sounds, the voice of someone who makes you feel safe or loved, city sounds, singing or playing an instrument, rhythmic sounds, white noise

Smell: nature, flowers, perfume, scented candles, tea, chocolate, essential oils, coffee, new-car smell, baking, fresh-cut grass, nostalgic scents that bring back happy memories

Taste: peppermint tea, chocolate, comfort food, something special you don't usually eat, savoring a flavor mindfully

Touch: cozy blankets or socks, favorite sweater, fidget toys, cold or warm compress, lotion, bath or shower, weighted blankets, petting your dog or cat, giving someone a hug, nonimpulsive physical intimacy

SELF-SOOTHING KIT

Create a self-soothing kit. Gather two or three items from each category—you're not limited to the items I listed. Get creative. Think of things that you already use or that are soothing to you. Gather the items in a box or bag or on an easily accessible shelf so that you can get to them when you need or want them. Use your kit regularly. Perhaps even make a second, portable kit to keep in your car or bag to take with you to school or work. Jot down some ideas here of what you might want to include in your self-soothing kit:

_____

_____

_____

SOOTHE YOUR SELF

In a moment when you're feeling some strong emotions, identify an emotion and rate it from 0 to 100. Write it down in your notebook. Choose one thing from each category/sense and use it to show yourself some kindness. After mindfully self-soothing, rate the emotion again. Write it in your notebook and write down your observations about the experience.

SURVIVING A CRISIS BY IMPROVE-ING THE MOMENT

There are moments that are so painful they feel intolerable. If we can change them or solve the problem, that is always the best way to go. However, there are times when we can't change the situation, or we can't change it yet. In situations like this, there are ways we can shift some dynamics of the moment to make it more tolerable. IMPROVE is an acronym that stands for imagery, meaning, prayer, relaxation, one thing in the moment, vacation, and encouragement. These IMPROVE techniques can help us see difficulties and ourselves in a slightly different light, which can make it easier to tolerate present discomfort. Some of these techniques shift our perspective on ourselves or the situation. Others change our bodies' responses, while yet others help us focus on accepting the moment while not clinging to it.

Although these skills that change or improve the moment can be overused, with intentionality they can help us cope until we figure out how else to deal with problems.

Imagery

With practice, you can use mental pictures, or visualization, to create a situation different from the one you're in right now—and one that is safe. This could be a safe room you've built inside your wise mind. It can be another place you've been to or would like to go to. Imagine designing a space where you can be safe from impulsive or destructive urges. What would you put in that space to protect you?

It is important to note that if you want to have access to this skill when in crisis, you must practice it frequently when you're not in crisis.

Meaning

It is an age-old belief that in order to survive suffering, it can be helpful to make meaning of our painful experiences. Some people find this meaning through their religious or spiritual perspectives. Others find it through helping other people out of similar experiences. Others may try to focus on what they are learning or ways in which they're growing stronger or more resilient through their struggles. Yet others find one small positive in an otherwise awful situation. The goal here is not to suggest that we should like our suffering. This skill simply gives you the option to slightly shift your perspective from abject misery to a sense that there is something bigger and that our suffering may not be completely in vain.

Prayer

In this context, prayer is similar to radical acceptance, which we will discuss in week 6. Prayer is being open to the moment that we are in, not the one we wish we were in. It's about asking for strength to get through the moment and being open to receiving it. It's not about escaping the pain of the moment, but rather getting through it, perhaps with the perspective that we are not alone in it. For some people, this means connecting to God; for others, it is a belief in a less-defined higher power, the universe, or humanity. This type of belief may be defined or still vague. Prayer can take many forms, and you can experiment with different kinds of prayers as you stay in the moment.

Relaxation

Relaxing actions aren't specific to structured relaxation exercises. Relaxing actions are activities you do that generally calm you down. When we are calm, it's easier for us to think clearly and make decisions that won't get us in trouble. What kinds of activities relax you? Perhaps watching a show, doing yoga, taking a bath/shower, breathing deeply, doing a craft, listening to a meditation, or drinking hot tea?

One Thing in the Moment

Returning to the "how" skill we learned in week 2 (page 37), focus on doing just one thing, one-mindfully. This skill requires practice. When you're overwhelmed, it can be difficult to focus. However, if you train yourself to focus on just one thing, it can really help you find some space and time to settle your feelings and thoughts. All you have to deal with is this one moment. It might be a painful one, but you can tolerate this pain by focusing all your attention on just . . . this . . . one . . . moment.

Vacation

Take a break from adulting for just a little while. Do something that allows you a retreat from the pain of the moment. Be sure to do this in a way that does not cause consequences later. For a short time—from a few minutes to no more than a day—take a time-out. This skill is not about running away or avoiding your responsibilities. It's an intentional moment to breathe and refuel, and to build up your reserves. This could be taking a nap, going to the woods, reading an enjoyable book, or turning your phone off for a while. Use this skill with purpose, not as a default. Give yourself a little vacation.

Encouragement

Be your own cheerleader. When someone you care about is struggling or doubting themself, what do you say? How do you validate and encourage them? How would you like someone else to encourage you? Do this for yourself. When you find yourself thinking that you can't cope or a situation is hopeless, give yourself a pep talk. This is not about artificially changing negative thinking to overly positive thinking. It's about giving yourself a realistic, believable boost. So instead of "I can't handle this," you might say, "I've got this." And if that doesn't feel believable, you might start with "I can try."

IMPROVE MY MOMENTS

Choose several activities in the previous section to practice. Try one per day three times this week and notice your emotions before and after the activity. Write down the emotion and score it out of 100 before and after the activity. Write down what you did and your experience with it. Keep trying each category of IMPROVE until you find the ones you like best. Then keep practicing them when you're *not* in distress so that you have access to them when you *are* in crisis. Continue to write down your experiences as you practice so that you can look back and see your progress. This will be an important part of learning to manage crises.

Emotion/Urge Before: ....

Emotion Rating (0 to 100): ....

IMPROVE Skill: ....

What I Actually Did: ....

Emotion Rating After (0 to 100): ....

Thoughts/Experiences: ....

....

REFRAMING SELF-DEFEAT

Identify three self-defeating statements that come up for you when you're struggling. Write down the statements, then write down a challenge or cheerleading statement that will help you shift your perspective when you're struggling with negative thoughts. Use the table to come up with your own.

NEGATIVE THOUGHT	CHALLENGE
I always screw up and do stupid things when I'm upset.	*I'm trying to slow down and think through things so I don't keep repeating mistakes.* *or* *I'm going to try something different.* *or* *I'm looking forward instead of backward.*

KEY TAKEAWAYS

As with all the DBT skills, we are rewiring our brain to not go down the same old rutted roads that we habitually travel when we're struggling. Distracting with Wise Minds ACCEPTS, Self-Soothing, and IMPROVE-ing the Moment will allow us to make choices when we're in a difficult moment that will not only *not* make things worse but also will increase our confidence and self-respect as we handle things well. Sometimes by soothing, distracting temporarily, or making the moment slightly better, we can decrease our distress enough to not have to do something drastic to tolerate the moment.

Key points from this chapter:

▶ Practice often.

▶ Buy yourself time, and respond instead of reacting.

▶ Try to stay with the moment, even when it's difficult.

▶ It's okay to take a break, but don't make a habit of avoiding.

Learning to Accept What You Cannot Change

There are things we have to accept as reality;
that doesn't mean we have to like them.

As we discussed in chapter 1, the main dialectic in DBT is acceptance and change. When people first come to DBT, we explain it this way: You likely have some ways of coping that you've developed over the years. There is no judgment for whatever you've done because it obviously worked, since you're still here. So we accept it, without exception—and at the same time, you wouldn't be here if you didn't feel something needed to change. Perhaps those same ways of coping are causing problems or aren't working so well anymore, so we are going to focus on helping you find some new ways to cope that don't add extra problems to the mix.

In this chapter, we will learn five different acceptance skills: radical acceptance, turning the mind, willingness, half smiling and willing hands, and mindfulness of current thoughts.

REALITY ACCEPTANCE

When people hear the terms *reality acceptance* and *radical acceptance*, there is often an instinct to push back, thinking that they're being told to "suck it up" or "get over it." That is not what reality acceptance is, though. Acceptance is not approval of our misery; it's not getting to a point of being okay with or liking our difficulties. Rather, it is acknowledging the facts and recognizing that when we refuse to accept our present reality for what it is, we add to our suffering. Without acceptance or acknowledgment of the facts, we can't move forward.

It can be a confusing concept, to be sure. Why would we use acceptance, then? There are several reasons that Linehan suggests:

▶ Refusing to accept it doesn't make it different.

▶ If we want to change things, we have to first know what we're dealing with.

▶ As much as we'd like to, we can't avoid pain.

▶ When we avoid or reject reality, our pain turns into suffering.

▶ Acceptance can bring freedom from bitterness.

▶ Though there may be sadness with acceptance, eventually there can be deep calm.

▶ We have to go through the pain to get out of it.

ACCEPTING REALITY

Think of something in your life that you have had a hard time accepting. It can be something simple, like a rainy day when you hoped for sun or having to be at school or work early when you're not a morning person. How would the situation be different if you accepted the facts?

Example:

Situation: *Rainy day*

How it would be different: *Would have carried an umbrella, not worn suede shoes*

Radical Acceptance

Radical acceptance is a life-perspective shift that goes far beyond surviving crises, and it also has practical implications for moments of pain and distress. Radical acceptance is reality acceptance, but deeper. To clarify the difference, *reality accep-tance* is acknowledging and conceding the facts of our current circumstances. *Radical acceptance* is full acceptance from a soul-deep level, including mind, heart, and body. Radical acceptance is for things that are very difficult to accept.

Radical acceptance is not giving up on changing the things that can change, having warm feelings for people who have hurt you, or approving of what we have experienced. It is rather accepting what is: that we all have limitations, that life is worthwhile even when there is pain, and that everything is caused—not to be confused with "everything happens for a reason"—and you just need to know the history to understand the why.

RADICAL ACCEPTANCE STEP-BY-STEP

This exercise is lengthy but can be returned to again and again when you are trying to move toward accepting something painful in your life. Note that skills from other weeks are mentioned. You can return to those chapters for reference.

1. Notice that you are pushing back or fighting reality. Remember what you're trying to accept. Describe the facts without judgment.

2. Remind yourself that this is the present reality. Make a statement that helps you adopt a mindset of acceptance, such as: "It is as it should be" (i.e., caused).

3. Analyze the causes of the reality you are trying to accept, looking into the past to understand what led to it.

4. Practice accepting with mind, body, and spirit—the whole self. Let go of the tension in your body so that you can let go of the refusal in your mind.

5. Practice opposite action (page 118). Instead of fighting the emotion, practice adopting an open posture. Imagine yourself accepting.

6. Cope ahead (page 112). Make a plan for coping with the feared emotions.

7. Notice any sensations that come up and approach them with curiosity, allowing them to be without judgment and then watching as they wane.

8. When sadness, disappointment, and grief come up, allow them to. Don't suppress them or allow anger to distract. Use crisis survival skills if needed.

9. Acknowledge that life is worthwhile, even with pain. Notice when you are fighting or judging pain, giving yourself space to notice and tolerate the pain.

10. Do pros and cons. Review the pros-and-cons exercise (page 60) and fill one out on acceptance.

Turning the Mind

When you find that your mind is wanting to refuse to accept, don't allow it to go there. Turn your mind *away* from nonacceptance and *toward* acceptance over and over and over again. Acceptance requires a choice or commitment to begin. Because the choice to accept sometimes only lasts a moment, we have to continually turn our minds back toward acceptance. Sometimes it is a small turn, and other times more like a full-body turn. By doing it again and again and again, we are forming that new pathway in our brain that will make it easier for us to travel down the path of acceptance.

CATCHING YOURSELF IN NONACCEPTANCE

It can be helpful to develop a plan for recognizing when you're in nonacceptance and then bringing yourself back to acceptance. Read the following example and then come up with a plan for your own scenario.

Example:

Situation: *I don't like the direction my supervisor at work has given me for a project, but she is not open to my feedback or to changing the project.*

Signs you're in nonacceptance: *Tight jaw and shoulders, irritability, wanting to quit, refusing to cooperate*

Judgmental or nonacceptance thoughts: *They don't know what they're talking about, it shouldn't be this way, I'm not going to do this, I can't handle this*

Reframes: *They want something different than I do, it is what it is, I can do this after I take a break, this is hard but I can do it*

Skills I can use from other weeks to help stay in the moment: *STOP, paced breathing, opposite action, mindfulness of something in my physical space around me, IMPROVE*

Now you give it a try:

Situation: ....

....

....

....

Signs you're in nonacceptance: ....

....

....

....

Judgmental or nonacceptance thoughts: ....

....

....

....

Reframes: ....

....

....

....

Skills I can use from other weeks to help stay in the moment: ....

....

....

....

Willfulness vs. Willingness

Willfulness is white-knuckling your way through life, digging in your heels and refusing to do what works, or looking for solutions because you think it "shouldn't be this way." Willingness is the opposite; it is accepting that things are the way they are and recognizing that fighting it isn't helping. Willingness is adopting a posture of acceptance and openness, sometimes literally with arms uncrossed and hands open. It is recognizing that fighting the facts and refusing to deal with reality won't get you anywhere except adding suffering to what's already painful enough.

MOVING FROM WILLFULNESS TO WILLINGNESS

Describe a situation in which you are being willful, digging in your heels, or refusing to do what needs to be done:

Ask yourself what the threat is in being willing:

Describe how you can radically accept your willfulness:

_____

_____

_____

_____

Now turn your mind toward willingness. Try adopting a willing posture and a half smile.

Half Smile and Willing Hands

Half smiling and willing hands are ways of using body and facial expressions to encourage acceptance. Sometimes when we can't quite get our minds there, our bodies and faces can help. Changing our facial expression from a grimace to a half smile and our clenched fists to open hands can send the message to our brain that we are open and accepting.

To half smile, relax your face from your forehead to your eyes, cheeks, mouth, and jaw. Notice the difference between that and a grimace. Then slightly tip the corners of your mouth up. It may not even be visible to another person, but you will feel it.

Willing hands is another way of using posture to encourage acceptance. It is also the opposite action (see week 9) for anger. Anger, which leads us to want to change something, is the opposite of acceptance, so adopting a posture that shifts anger can open us to acceptance. Unclenching the fists, opening the fingers, and laying the hands, palms up, is what we mean by _willing hands_.

HALF SMILE WITH WILLING HANDS

It is difficult to maintain anger when using these skills. Think of something that makes you feel some anger. While thinking about it, notice your facial expression, muscles, and your posture. Relax your face completely and then tip the corners of your mouth up slightly. You can even look in the mirror to see that it's barely visible. As you half smile, unclench your hands, open your fingers, and face your palms up. Relax your shoulders. Breathe. Notice whether you are able to maintain the anger at the same level, and record your experience in your notebook.

Mindfulness of Current Thoughts

To be mindful of our thoughts is to accept them without judgment, to accept that they are simply temporary sensations that come and go. Our tendency is to treat thoughts as facts and to react immediately to them or to jump on board and follow them wherever they go. However, if we observe and accept them as momentary sensations, we can choose to have a different relationship to our thoughts. We often think we must change our thoughts in order to reduce the pain they lead to, but by accepting them for what they are we can reduce the pain without changing or suppressing the thoughts.

CHOOSING YOUR THOUGHTS

Set a timer for 20 seconds. During that time, observe any thoughts that arise. After the timer goes off, shift your thoughts to what you did today. Review the activities from the time you woke up until now, including getting out of bed, brushing your teeth, getting ready for the day . . . all the way until this moment.

Notice that in the first part of your exercise you observed your thoughts and in the second you chose your thoughts. Reflect on the difference between the two experiences.

KEY TAKEAWAYS ....

Acceptance is one of the more challenging skills we teach in DBT. It can be emotionally difficult to allow ourselves to accept painful circumstances when everything in us wants to push back and say, "It's not fair!" To be clear, all we are being asked to accept are facts about the past and present and reasonable understanding of limitations about the future, such as not qualifying to be president of the United States if you were not born in the United States or not being able to be a professional athlete if you aren't athletic. We often expect ourselves to accept distortions, such as "I was doomed from the beginning" or "I will always be alone."

As we try to move toward acceptance, there are skills to help us. Some skills, such as turning the mind and mindfulness of current thoughts, help us accept with our minds. Half smiling and willing hands help us accept with our bodies. Radical acceptance and willingness help us accept with mind, body, and spirit.

Key points from this chapter:

▸ Acceptance is not approval.

▸ Acceptance is a process.

▸ Acceptance is required for and can lead to change.

▸ Willingness is more effective than willfulness at getting us what we want.

Getting to Know Your Emotions Using Emotion Regulation

Having emotions is part of being human—for better or worse—and really, it's better.

One of the primary reasons people seek out DBT is that they feel ruled by their emotions and the urges that go along with having big, overwhelming emotions. They hope that therapy can help them stop having so many emotions. But emotions are an important part of our life experience, so the goal is not to shut them down, as tempting as that might seem. It has been said that DBT is a therapy of emotional experiencing, and that is truly one of our primary goals: to be able to experience the fullness of our emotions without feeling ruled by them. We want to live our lives and not just survive them. The skills that we will focus on for the next couple of weeks will help us understand, navigate, and manage—or regulate—our emotions.

WHAT IS EMOTION REGULATION?

Regulating emotions means being able to have some control over your emotions: which ones you experience, when and how intensely you experience them, and how you act on or express them. Emotion regulation skills help us understand and identify our emotions accurately, have unwanted emotions less often, suffer less because of difficult emotions, and be less vulnerable to emotion mind, which we'll discuss in this section. It's important to remember that emotions are not good or bad; they just *are*. We only want to regulate, or decrease, ineffective emotions. If emotions are serving an important function, such as sending a message or motivating ourselves or others in a way that will benefit us, then we don't want to get rid of them entirely. Pretending emotions aren't there or suppressing them may make us feel better in the moment but generally only delays dealing with the problem, and often the problem is worse later.

The Three Thinking Styles

In week 1, we learned about wise mind, which is a balance between reasonable mind and emotion mind. As we think about emotion regulation skills, one of their primary functions is to help us be less inclined to make decisions from emotion mind and to get into wise mind more easily. Making decisions in wise mind gives us a balanced approach to life, whereas making decisions solely based on emotions will often get us in trouble. Let's briefly review emotion mind, reasonable mind, and wise mind, which we learned about in week 1.

The Reasoning Self

In reasonable mind, we are often clinical and detached. We disregard emotions. We make decisions based on intellect and facts and what we deem rational. When we are planning or following technical directions, we are in reasonable mind. This can be useful for some situations, but if we continually exclude emotions—ours and others'—we will be detached and unbalanced.

The Emotional Self

When we are in emotion mind, we are making decisions based on feelings to the exclusion of facts or reason. Sometimes we think we're focusing on facts but because of our high level of emotions, the facts are distorted—either minimized or exaggerated. As was mentioned in week 1, sometimes we need to act on emotions. Other times we want to act on them, such as when we are expressing intense love. Often, though, acting on emotions means making impulsive decisions that we might regret once the intensity of the emotions comes down.

The Wise Self

When we are in our wise mind, we are more than emotion and reason. Wise mind takes both into account and becomes something more. Do you remember when we learned about dialectics in chapter 1? We learned that a dialectic includes the best of both opposing sides and then adds to both. If wise mind is a dialectic, then we recognize that shutting down emotions does not get us to balance or a synthesis of emotion and reason. Emotion and reason are both needed to get to a wise state of being.

BREATHING INTO WISE MIND

While we all have a wise mind inherent to our being, accessing it can be challenging at first. There are many exercises to help you practice accessing your wise mind. A simple one that you can practice easily is to focus on your breath.

Find a comfortable, well-supported position and settle in. Turn your attention to your breath as you breathe in and out gently. Follow the rhythm of your breath, all the way through the inhale and all the way through the exhale. If you get distracted, just notice that and bring your attention back. Eventually, tune in your focus to the very bottom of your inhale, finding your physical center. Wise mind is not an actual physical place, but many people find that focusing on the center point of their body helps them connect to their "gut," or wise mind. The more you practice finding it, the easier it will get.

FINDING WISE MIND

See if you can identify an emotion that you are feeling right now. Name the emotion and notice what it feels like in your body. Identify a physical sensation and see if you can follow it as you allow the emotion to come and go. Notice whether the sensation changes. Is there an urge attached to this emotion? What is it? Now ask wise mind a question: "Would it be wise mind to act on this urge?" Once you've asked the question, wait quietly for an answer. You won't always get one immediately, but the more you ask and listen, the easier it will get to find the wise-minded answer.

Emotion(s):

Bodily sensation(s):

Urge(s):

Is it wise mind?

If yes, what is the wise-minded action?

If no, what would wise mind do?

GETTING TO KNOW YOUR EMOTIONS

Emotions, as we've noted, can make us feel like we're on a roller coaster or in an out-of-control car and we aren't the ones driving. Especially when emotions are big and overwhelming, it can seem like we have no control at all over them. We will be learning about various ways to manage our emotions, but we will be well on our way to having some control just by understanding what emotions are and what they do. Simply identifying and naming an emotion will often cause its intensity to go down just a little bit. Having language to describe our emotions is an important skill if we hope to understand and manage them.

The What, How, and Why of Emotions

What are emotions? Why do we call them *feelings*? Emotions are sensations that originate in the brain. They are sudden and involuntary, and they produce sensations in the body. As Dr. Linehan is known for saying, "We call them feelings because we feel them in our bodies." Often we notice the physical sensations before we are even aware we are experiencing an emotion.

Emotions serve several important functions. These functions include acting as a warning system, motivating us to action, and communicating to both ourselves and others.

It is said that an emotion itself lasts up to 90 seconds but that the body's response to a single emotion can last up to about 20 minutes unless we attend to or feed it. If we feed or perpetuate it, it can become a mood, which can last a lot longer.

Being able to categorize our emotions is the beginning of having some mastery over them.

CATEGORIZING YOUR EMOTIONS

In DBT, we focus on 10 major categories of emotions. Most are self-explanatory, but a few require a little clarification. Those that are commonly understood are fear, anger, sadness, happiness, and love. The ones that require some clarifying in terms of the way we define them in DBT are as follows:

- **Guilt** is when something you've done or a characteristic you have violates your own moral code.

- ▸ **Shame** is when your action or trait puts you at risk of rejection by a social group whose approval matters to you.
- ▸ **Envy** is wanting what someone else has.
- ▸ **Jealousy** is the feeling of insecurity that something or someone of yours might be threatened or you might lose it.
- ▸ **Disgust** is a strong dislike or revulsion for something or someone. Shame can't exist without disgust.

In your notebook, write down each of the 10 categories of emotions. List as many synonyms or subcategories of emotions as you can for each. This will help you see the range and subtleties of emotions. Not all irritation is rage, and not all appreciation for people is undying love.

Primary vs. Secondary Emotions

Primary and *secondary emotions* refer to the order in which we experience emotions. Imagine that you go out somewhere in public and realize that you are still wearing your fuzzy slippers. The initial emotion you might experience would likely be surprise, then maybe embarrassment or amusement, perhaps shame, and maybe eventually anger. The surprise or embarrassment, if they came first, would be the primary emotion. Everything else would be secondary. Secondary emotions are typically a response to the primary ones. We might be angry because embarrassment is too uncomfortable, or we might feel ashamed because we believe we are socially unacceptable for making a mistake. It can be helpful to be aware of secondary emotions because they don't always fit the situation we are responding to.

EXPLORING PRIMARY AND SECONDARY EMOTIONS

Think of a time when you've had more than one emotion in response to a situation. Write down the emotions that you experienced. Which do you think was primary (the one that was a direct response to the situation)? Which was secondary, and how do you think you got there? Think about what the emotions felt like. Where did you feel them in your body?

Situation: ....

Emotions: ....

Rating (0 to 100): ....

Primary emotion: ....

Secondary emotion: ....

Bodily sensations: ....

KEY TAKEAWAYS ....

Emotion regulation is at the core of DBT. Understanding how our emotions function and developing the language and awareness to identify them accurately is
key to learning to shift them, as well as to experience them without feeling ruled
by them. Being able to identify and name primary and secondary emotions is a
first step to having a positive relationship with our emotions.

Key points from this chapter:

▸ Everyone has all the same emotions.

▸ We don't want to shut down our emotions completely; suppressing them
  only delays having to deal with them as they'll keep coming back.

▸ Emotions serve three functions: They communicate to ourselves, communicate to others, and motivate action.

▸ We don't have to be ruled by our emotions.

Understanding Emotional Dysregulation

Emotions aren't good or bad; they just are.

This week, you will get some additional background on how we make sense of the patterns we are addressing with DBT skills. The modules of DBT are specifically designed to treat each area of dysregulation mentioned in this chapter. As emotion regulation has long been considered the hallmark or foundational area of dysregulation, it makes sense to look at where it comes from as we further explore the emotion regulation module.

In the therapy world, we work hard to be sure the treatment we are providing is the right approach to the specific problems we are trying to treat. In other words, we want to be sure that the treatment we are using actually works for the problems we're having. The information in this chapter—the biosocial theory, the five areas of dysregulation, and the description of chain analysis as a way to understand the links among emotions, thoughts, and actions—will help you be sure that these skills and concepts are designed to assist you effectively.

THE BIOSOCIAL THEORY

The biosocial theory is Linehan's theory of how borderline personality disorder (BPD) develops, and DBT as a treatment is designed to address the problematic patterns that develop when people have these kinds of experiences. While many people who benefit from DBT do not meet criteria for BPD, many of us can relate to feeling overwhelmed by emotions and being misunderstood or invalidated. Thus, the skills of DBT are relevant far beyond a diagnosis.

The biosocial theory suggests that some people just have bigger emotions than others and that this is biological—they're either born that way or some other physical experiences, such as disease or addiction, have shifted their wiring to be more sensitive and reactive. Having big emotions on its own is not necessarily a problem. However, when you place a person with big emotions in what we call an *invalidating environment*, where they're responded to as if their reactions are inaccurate, inappropriate, or wrong, they're made to feel like they are the problem just for being themselves. Various environments can function as invalidating—abuse, neglect, addiction, racism, classism, homophobia, bullying, and other egregious dynamics can all create invalidating environments. However, it can also be what we call a poorness of fit. Many times families are doing their best to take care of and support the child, but the child still experiences the world as a terrifying place.

According to very recent DBT research, our views of the core characteristics of BPD may be shifting as findings suggest that sensitivity to interpersonal distress may be even more central than biological sensitivity to big emotions. DBT continues to shift and adapt as we continue to learn.

The Five Areas of Dysregulation

One of the fundamentally unique aspects of Linehan's work is the way she reorganized our understanding of BPD. She helped us shift from viewing it as flawed wiring in someone's personality to seeing patterns of behavior that make sense when you understand how and why they developed. The hallmark characteristic, she suggested, was a pervasive pattern of emotion dysregulation, with the other four areas of dysregulation stemming from it. In this section, we will define the five areas of dysregulation. These can be experienced by anyone, not just those with BPD. Linehan suggested that for people with BPD, dysregulation shows up across all areas of life. Research continues to show us that the interaction between interpersonal conflict and overwhelming emotions is transactional—in other words, they feed off each other—and this leads to developing ways of coping that help us avoid pain in the short term but may not be effective in the long run.

Each skill module in DBT is designed to help develop skills in these areas of deficit as follows.

Emotion Dysregulation

Pervasive patterns of emotion dysregulation show up in the form of high sensitivity and big reactions when emotions are provoked. People can seem like their emotions are all over the place, swinging from all to nothing or hot to cold in no time. Emotions in general are big and intense, and it's not uncommon for anger to be a big part of the mix. This is related to the challenges that people have with seeing emotions as a moment in time or relational reactions as temporary.

The emotion regulation module is designed to help build skills in understanding and managing emotions, as well as being able to experience them without being overwhelmed or ruled by them.

Interpersonal Dysregulation

As you'd imagine, when a person's emotions are big and intense, or experienced as chaotic, that is going to show up in their relationships. Relationships and patterns of connection can be equally chaotic. Often other people struggle to know how to deal with the emotional roller coaster. In reality, those people often leave, whether literally or just emotionally. As a result, a completely understandable fear of abandonment often develops and then continues to interfere with relationships.

In the interpersonal effectiveness module, the focus is on building skills to effectively ask for what we need or to say no to requests while still maintaining relationships and self-respect.

Self-Dysregulation

This area has to do with having a dysregulated or insecure/unstable sense of self. When the target of understanding self in relationship to how others respond is a moving one, it can be difficult to see the parts of self that don't change even when relationships do. In adults, this can show up as a chronic sense of emptiness. In adolescents, it often looks like a sense of perpetual boredom or lack of interest or an absence of caring even when there is plenty to do.

Core mindfulness skills are key in helping a person learn to experience reality and themselves as they are, independent of the waves of opinion, past and future worries, judgments, and changing relationships.

Behavioral Dysregulation

When a person experiences frequent emotional chaos, it's not unlikely that impulsive actions will follow in an attempt to escape or avoid the emotions. Self-injury, substance abuse, risky sex, shoplifting, reckless driving, and other behaviors are common.

Distress tolerance skills help us survive crises without using these impulsive behaviors. We build our confidence in being able to tolerate discomfort instead of escaping or avoiding it, and we also learn the power of acceptance in decreasing our suffering.

Cognitive Dysregulation

Cognitive dysregulation refers to dissociative and paranoid thought processes. Rigid, black and white, and inflexible thinking are other examples of this. Dissociation is a mental process of detachment that develops when life is just "too much." It's a protective mechanism to keep our minds and systems from being overloaded. It's something we want to get away from long term, but it is a completely understandable thing when life has been overwhelming.

Distress tolerance skills also help in coping with the intensity of cognitive distress.

EXPLORING THE FIVE AREAS OF DYSREGULATION

Put some thought into whether these five areas show up in your life. Is there one that feels most applicable? Do experiences in one area tend to lead into experiences in another? For example, does emotional chaos lead into questions about your sense of self or impulsive behaviors? Or do interpersonal conflicts lead to emotional ups and downs? Write down your thoughts in your notebook.

WHAT'S MY EXPERIENCE?

If it is not too distressing to ponder, write down the aspects of the biosocial theory that feel applicable to you. Thinking about the past can sometimes lead to difficult emotions. If thinking about the biosocial theory distresses you, consider having this conversation with a therapist. Use some self-soothing skills to help you with the discomfort. Refer back to week 4 for some ideas on how to self-soothe.

THE LINK BETWEEN EMOTIONS AND BEHAVIORS

As we discussed in the previous chapter, being able to identify and understand the emotions we're experiencing is the beginning of learning to manage them. Just identifying and labeling an emotion makes it decrease in intensity a little bit. Understanding the relationships among our emotions, responses, and actions can have an even larger impact on our ability to gain some control over our patterns of behavior. Remember, in behavioral therapy, emotions, thoughts, actions, and body sensations are all considered behaviors. Let's clarify a bit about how emotions lead to actions and how we might use this understanding to decrease some of our problematic behaviors and increase some of the skillful ones.

How Emotions Become Actions

Have you ever heard someone say "You make me so mad" or "That makes me so sad"? It's not uncommon that we think a situation or another person's actions cause emotions or behaviors, but it's actually more complicated than that. One of our primary tools in DBT for understanding the link between our emotions and actions is chain analysis. In chain analysis, we look at the links in a chain of external and internal dynamics to understand how we got from an event to an action or behavior. It's the way we perceive or interpret the event that leads to our emotions (brain/body changes) Then those changes lead to urges, which often lead to actions that cause problematic consequences. Let's look at an example.

Here's what a chain looks like:

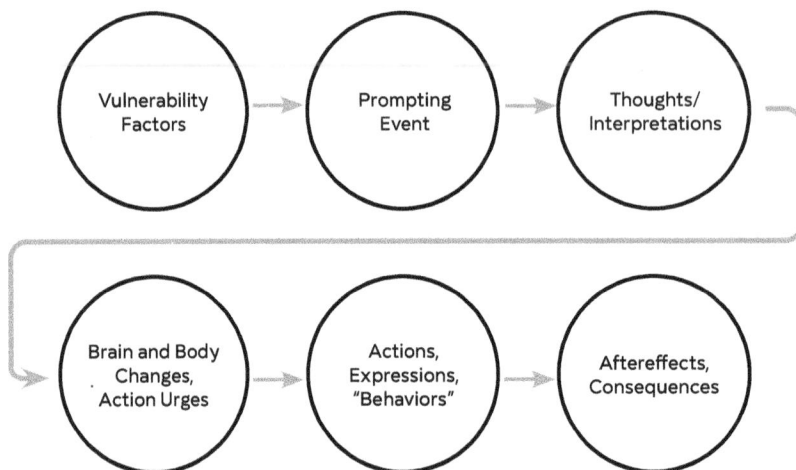

Vulnerability Factors → Prompting Event → Thoughts/Interpretations → Brain and Body Changes, Action Urges → Actions, Expressions, "Behaviors" → Aftereffects, Consequences

In DBT, there is an expression: "What we track changes." As we track emotions, urges, and behaviors on a diary card, we begin to see patterns of emotions, urges, and the resulting emotions we experience after we use the target behaviors we are trying to change. Often the target behavior we are trying to change is not actually the problem; it's the attempt to solve the problem. In order to stop the behavior, we need to find another way to solve the problem that led to using the behavior. In the chart on page 103, the wine and angry texting are attempts to solve the problem of feeling bad because of ongoing family conflict.

CHAIN ANALYSIS: FIGURING OUT WHAT HAPPENED

Think of a time an event led to a behavior you're trying to change. (Choose an incident that won't bring up unmanageable emotions.) Can you identify what happened between the prompting event and the action or behavior? What were you thinking? What were you feeling? What were you experiencing in your body? Were there vulnerability factors, such as being extra tired or already stressed? Write down everything you can remember about what happened between the prompting event and the action, and also what happened after. Did you feel relieved initially? Did your support system respond in a certain way? Did you spiral into shame or self-blame? If you get stuck, ask yourself, "What happened next?"

There's not one right way to do this, but here's an example of what a chain might look like. Use the blank chart on page 104 to try your own chain or re-create it in your notebook. Exploring your chains, over and over and over, can give you great insight into what might need to shift in order to change the behavior. Once you've filled it out, go back and circle the things that seem like they most contributed to using the target behavior.

VULNERABILITY FACTORS	PROMPTING EVENT	THOUGHTS, BELIEFS, INTERPRETATIONS
Didn't get much sleep last night Have a cold Stressed at work	Argument with my sister about helping our mom with her house	I can't handle this It's not fair They all expect me to do everything No one cares about my life I don't have time right now I can't ever get it right

EMOTIONS, SENSATIONS, URGES	ACTIONS, EXPRESSIONS, BEHAVIORS	AFTEREFFECTS, CONSEQUENCES
Feeling tense, shoulders tight Fists clenched Heaviness in belly Sad Mad Guilty	Drink a bottle of wine and send angry text to sister	Relief for a little while Guilt about text Shame about drinking Spiral into self-hatred Sister's feelings are hurt Mom worried

VULNERABILITY FACTORS	PROMPTING EVENT	THOUGHTS, BELIEFS, INTERPRETATIONS

EMOTIONS, SENSATIONS, URGES	ACTIONS, EXPRESSIONS, BEHAVIORS	AFTEREFFECTS, CONSEQUENCES

MISSING LINKS ANALYSIS—WHAT COULD HAVE HELPED?

In chain analysis, we ask the question "What happened?" in order to figure out how we got to the problem behavior. On the flip side of a chain is what's called a *missing links analysis*, where we ask, "What would have been effective?" In order to figure out what would have helped us be effective in the situation, we ask the following questions. The examples are from the same scenario we used for our chain analysis exercise.

Remember, the goal isn't to make us feel guilt or shame about what we did wrong. It's to help us figure out how to be more effective in the future.

Example:

Did I know what effective behavior would've helped?

_____ Yes ___X___ No

If no, what got in the way?
I was tired and emotional and acted without thinking.
How could I have problem-solved?
I could've told my sister I was tired and asked to talk in the morning.

Was I willing to do what was needed?

_____ Yes ___X___ No

If no, what got in the way of being willing?
I was annoyed with my sister and didn't want to cooperate.

Did the thought of being effective even occur to me?

_____ Yes ___X___ No

If no, how could I problem-solve so I'm more likely to think of ways to be skillful?
I can practice the skills more that could help (like STOP), practice my interpersonal effectiveness skills, take a little time before responding to her texts.

Give this a try with your own situation:

Did I know what effective behavior would've helped?

_____ Yes _____ No

If no, what got in the way?

....

....

How could I have problem-solved?

....

....

Was I willing to do what was needed?

_____Yes _____ No

If no, what got in the way of being willing?

....

....

Did the thought of being effective even occur to me?

_____Yes _____ No

If no, how could I problem-solve so I'm more likely to think of ways to be skillful?

....

....

KEY TAKEAWAYS ....

In this chapter, we looked at the theory that has driven our understanding of how borderline personality disorder develops and how it shows up in people's lives. We also looked at a model of how events lead to thoughts and interpretations, then to body changes and emotions, and finally to actions. I introduced you to the basics of chain analysis and the role it can have in changing patterns of behavior that aren't working for you anymore.

Key points from this chapter:
- ▶ It is the interaction of emotional sensitivity and an invalidating environment that leads to problematic emotion-driven behaviors.
- ▶ Emotions aren't good or bad; they just are.
- ▶ Events don't cause emotions and action urges; interpretations of the events do.
- ▶ It's not easy, but by analyzing your emotions and behaviors you can move toward changing them.

Decreasing Your Emotional Vulnerability and Changing Emotional Responses

Emotions sometimes feel like they're never going to end, but they will change, and we can change them.

Regulating emotions is not just about changing or decreasing emotions once they've come up, though we will learn skills for that. A key component in emotional balance, or managing the ups and downs we all have, is decreasing our vulnerability to emotions before they even arise. The more equilibrium we have in our lives, the less overwhelmed we will get when challenges come up. Then the emotions that do come up will be within our ability to manage and to only act on when necessary or appropriate.

In this chapter, we will look at specific skills for decreasing the likelihood of big reactions, and we will also learn some skills for bringing down intense emotions. First, let's figure out what makes us more or less resilient in the first place.

USING ABC PLEASE

One of the most important ways we can build our resilience to emotions is by living a life that we experience as worth living. When we're living a meaningful life by our own standards, the hard things get put into perspective. It's a combination of the events and circumstances of our lives as well as our responses to them that contributes to our happiness or the lack thereof. This also includes taking care of our bodies, as our physical well-being contributes to our resilience.

The ABC PLEASE skills give some practical ways to begin, or continue, to build this kind of life. The ABC part of the acronym includes skills that are designed to help us reduce our vulnerability to emotion mind by accumulating positive experiences to balance the hard ones, building a sense of accomplishment and mastery, and coping ahead of time when we know hard things are coming up. The PLEASE part of the acronym focuses on taking care of our physical bodies so that we are more resilient to challenging emotions and difficulties in life. The body and the mind/emotions are inextricably linked. If your body is out of balance, you will be more vulnerable to negative emotions and more likely to make decisions out of emotion mind.

Accumulate Positives

We all have responsibilities that take energy and resources, and we all have some painful experiences. In order to balance those, we also need a mixture of short-term positive or pleasant events to produce positive emotions, long-term meaningful experiences, and positive movement toward our goals and values. We need to deposit things in our emotional bank accounts and not just withdraw from them. To do that, we must:

1. Accumulate positives short term: It's important to have positive experiences that produce positive emotions and balance the negative ones. Accumulating positives also counters the tendency to avoid all experiences in an attempt to avoid negative ones. That only keeps us from having positive ones, too.

2. Accumulate positives long term: All lives are worth living, but when we are trying to improve our own lives, it's important to fill them with things that are meaningful to us and fit with our own values and priorities. Note that values can shift and change over time.

3. Once we know our values and priorities, we need to set goals and take action toward them.

DEFINE YOUR PERSONAL VALUES

The exploration of personal values that guide us in life is beyond the space we have in this book, but here's a place to start. Mark off as many of these values as feel important to you. Add your own if they're not on the list. Then narrow the list down to five. Next, narrow it down to one or two and choose one for the next step in this exercise.

☐ Relationships
☐ Belonging in a group
☐ Having power and influence
☐ Achieving things
☐ Pleasure and satisfaction
☐ Excitement and newness
☐ Being respectful
☐ Being self-directed

☐ Being spiritual
☐ Being secure
☐ Seeing the good in all
☐ Contributing to a cause
☐ Self-development
☐ Integrity
☐ ....
☐ ....

Once you've narrowed it down to a few values, choose one to take action on. Write down three things you can do to move toward your value.

Value to work toward: ....

Three possible actions: ....

....

....

Choose one action to take today: ....

Build Mastery

We all need to feel capable. Learning new things and building new abilities, or a sense of mastery, is an important part of having a life worth living. As a matter of fact, as long as we are alive, our brains are capable of learning new things. As we move toward later adulthood, we have a tendency to not place ourselves in new situations in which we can have the opportunity to learn new things. We also do this when we allow anxiety and avoidance to rule. It's important to intentionally do things to build a sense of accomplishment. We should look for ways to challenge ourselves but not to defeat ourselves. Building the difficulty level over time is key.

Imagine yourself as a pole vaulter. Clearing the bar on the highest setting might be too difficult for now, but you'll be able to work your way up to it with time and practice.

TRY NEW THINGS

Identify and write down ahead of time one thing to try each day, at least three times this week. They can be separate things or steps toward a larger goal. Do something that is challenging but possible: not too easy, not too difficult. Setting tasks that are too easy won't give you a sense of accomplishment; those that are too difficult set you up for frustration. Gradually increasing the level of difficulty keeps you moving forward. When you succeed with each step, no matter how small, celebrate it.

Keep track of your accomplishments and come back to them when you need a boost.

Cope Ahead

Cope ahead is a skill for when you know you have a challenging situation coming up. It has three parts: planning for how to cope effectively with expected difficulties, imagining being in the situation and handling it skillfully or effectively, and relaxing afterward to make an association with skillfulness and confidence. Imagining is just as important as having a plan, because you are firing new connections in the part of the brain that will use the plan, and essentially wiring confidence before you even get in the situation. Similar to the mental practice that we discussed earlier in the book (page 16), relaxation is an important component of this skill.

PREPARE AND PRACTICE

In your notebook, identify a scenario for which you'd like to cope ahead. Is it a family gathering? Presentation? Job interview? Next, follow these instructions:

▶ Name the emotions and urges that might come up and make it tough to use your skills.

▶ Decide the skills or techniques you will use.

▶ Imagine yourself in the situation, in present tense, in great detail.

▶ Rehearse the scenario out loud, walking through the situation from start to finish and being skillful. Practice coping with various situations or problems that might come up, including the worst-case scenario. You can also write this part down like a script and use it to rehearse aloud.

▶ Practice relaxation techniques after your rehearsal. (Don't skip this part!)

Physical Illness

If you have any physical illness, whether temporary like a cold, a long-term illness, or chronic pain, this can make it even harder to deal with emotional difficulties. Doing all you can to treat and manage disease or pain increases your resistance to emotional difficulty.

(BaLanced) Eating

Determining what kinds of foods and eating schedule make you feel good over time is important. This includes not eating too much or too little, avoiding spikes in blood sugar, and avoiding foods that make you feel bad physically or emotionally. This can be challenging if you have a complicated relationship with food, but it is important to have a consistent plan.

Avoiding Mood-Altering Substances

It can be tempting to use illicit drugs or alcohol to manage or avoid emotional stress, but using them actually decreases our ability to resist negative emotions and often increases negative emotions over time. Dependence on substances to manage emotions can lead to addiction.

(Balanced) <u>S</u>leep

A consistent sleep schedule and amount of sleep increases your resilience. This is especially important if you're struggling to sleep or dealing with depression. Too much or too little sleep has negative effects on physical, mental, and emotional health. Try to go to bed and wake up at the same time every day and refrain from looking at screens right before bed.

<u>E</u>xercise

Movement is important. It helps us get unstuck from our emotions. If it's accessible for you, consistent exercise is key. We know that 20 minutes of aerobic exercise five to seven days a week can achieve great results and act as an antidepressant. If that is not possible for you, you can likely still do some form of stretching or movement. Even getting outside for a bit can give you some of the benefits.

CHANGING UNWANTED EMOTIONS

Our first-choice response to any situation that produces difficult emotions is to solve the problem leading to the emotion. Only when we can't solve the problem do we turn to other skills like changing emotions. The skills in this section are for changing unwanted emotions, which would include emotions that don't fit the facts, emotions that are ineffective at moving you toward your goals, and emotions that fit but are too intense for the situation. First, we will learn to identify and name our emotions. Then we will learn how to determine whether our emotions fit the facts of the situation. Finally, we will learn how to use opposite action to get ineffective or unwanted emotions to come down.

Note: For the exercises in this section, we will follow the same scenario through each of the skills.

Identify and Name Your Emotion

As mentioned in the previous chapter, it's a skill simply to be able to name an emotion. As we aim to regulate our emotions, knowing exactly what we're feeling and what is leading to our feelings is important. The more specific we can get with identifying our emotions and their prompts, the better able we will be to change them. Try the following exercise to help you achieve a clearer under-standing of how to accurately identify the emotion(s) you are experiencing.

IDENTIFYING AND LABELING EMOTIONS

In the space provided, identify an emotion that you are experiencing and rate it on a scale of 0 to 100. Then write down body sensations, body language, or urges you're feeling along with the emotion.

Next, write down what you think was the prompting event for the emotion. Identify as many synonyms or subcategories of that emotion as you can come up with. Finally, determine whether one of these synonyms fits your experience better. Now rate the intensity of your emotion again. A completed version of this exercise is included here to help you get started.

Emotion: Fear

Rating (0 to 100): 55

Body sensations/language: Heart sped up, tense muscles, breathing fast, arms crossed, hunched, want to run or get away

Prompting event: Not wanting to be at a party with co-workers

Synonyms: Worry, anxiety, concern, embarrassment, scared, shy

New emotion name: Anxiety, shyness

Rating (0 to 100): 45

Emotion: ....

Rating (0 to 100): ....

Body sensations/language: ....

Prompting event: ....

Synonyms: ....

New emotion name: ....

Rating (0 to 100): ....

Check the Facts

Sometimes we want to change our emotions. Before we can do that, we need to check the facts. This doesn't mean that we are questioning whether we should feel the way we do. Checking the facts means determining whether an emotion fits the facts of the situation. As we learned in week 8, our emotions are responses to our *interpretations* of events. Sometimes gathering the facts can influence or change our interpretations, which can then change our emotions or at least let us know it makes sense to change our emotions. Assuming that our interpretations or thoughts are correct can sometimes lead to extreme emotions or additional problems.

FACT-CHECKING YOUR EMOTIONS

Ask yourself the following questions and record your answers in the space provided:

▸ What is the emotion I want to change? Rate it out of 100.
▸ What event prompted the emotion?
▸ What are my interpretations of the event?
▸ Am I assuming a threat? Label it. (Often strong or painful emotions come from a sense of threat or concern about possible negative outcomes.)
▸ Identify other possible outcomes.
▸ What's the worst-case scenario if the threat happens? (Usually, it's not as bad as our fear.) And what's more likely?
▸ Does my emotion or its intensity fit the facts?

Emotion I want to change: ....

Rating (0 to 100): ....

Prompting event: ....

My interpretations: ....

Possible threat: ....

Other possible outcomes: ....

Worst-case scenario/likely scenario: ....

Does my emotion or its intensity fit the facts? ....

Determine Your Action Urge and What You Want as a Result

Emotions have hardwired action urges associated with them. The urge of fear, for example, is to run or avoid. The urge of anger is to attack. The urge of love is to embrace. Sometimes acting on these urges makes sense and is absolutely appropriate, such as wanting to get away when faced with a roaring lion. Other times acting on the urges immediately will get us in trouble or at least is unnecessary. If we've checked the facts and determined that either our emotion or its intensity doesn't fit the facts of the situation, we will probably not want to act on the urge. It's also possible that we'll need to put off acting on the urge in the moment or situation we're in. Deciding whether to act on an urge might be determined by whether the likely outcome of the action matches what we are hoping to accomplish.

EXAMINING YOUR URGES

Let's consider what the urge might be in your scenario. Look at the examples in the box and then answer these questions in the space provided:

EMOTIONS	ACTION URGE
Fear	Run away/avoid
Anger	Attack
Sadness	Withdraw/isolate
Shame	Hide/avoid
Love	Embrace

What is the emotion you are having?

What is the urge you are having attached to your emotion?

Will it be effective to act on it right now?

Connect with Your Wise Mind: How Does Your Urge Move You Toward or Away from Your Goal?

Last week, we reviewed the three states of mind—reasonable, emotional, and wise—and I explained that accessing wise mind requires practice. The more we practice tuning into wise mind, the more we will be able to rely on our ability to make balanced, wise-minded decisions rather than emotional ones. In the context of determining whether to act on urges, wise mind can help us decide whether it's effective.

ASK WISE MIND A QUESTION

If you're still unsure of whether to act on the urge, ask wise mind a question: "Will expressing this emotion or acting on it be helpful or effective in this situation?"

Record the wise-minded answer to the question. If you aren't sure yet, give it some time and wait for an answer. Waiting has the added benefit of buying you time to decide whether it makes sense to act. Practicing this will help you to eventually be able to act in wise mind more easily.

Acting Opposite to Your Urges

Now that we've checked the facts and determined the urges attached, opposite action may be the next step. If our emotions and urges fit the facts and are appropriate to the moment, then we've acted on them. If we've decided that acting on them won't get us where we want to go, though, we may need opposite action. Opposite action is a biological skill that actually helps us change our brain chemistry. As we've discussed elsewhere in the book, our bodies can communicate to our brains. By doing the opposite of the urge, the emotions will begin to come down.

When doing opposite action, be sure to let the action do the heavy lifting of changing emotions. Don't shove down or suppress the emotion at the same time. Let the opposite action do the work.

DETERMINING OPPOSITE ACTION

Remember that opposite action is for when you've already determined the emotion is not justified, and therefore you don't want to act on it. In our example of the work party (page 115), the emotion is fear. Anxiety, as a form of fear, fits the facts, but the intensity doesn't. If the action urge is to run or avoid, the opposite action would be to approach, or to go to the party anyway. The techniques listed in the opposite action column are the actions that will produce the biological changes that bring the emotions down. The way you do these things can vary depending on your circumstances. After reading the table, answer the questions that follow.

EMOTION	URGE/ACTION (IF JUSTIFIED)	OPPOSITE ACTION
Fear	Freeze, run, avoid, get control	Do what you're afraid of repeatedly, approach
Anger	Fight back, avoid, overcome obstacles	Gently avoid, be kind, try to understand the other person
Disgust	Remove, clean up, influence others, avoid or push away	Go near, be kind, imagine things from the other person's perspective
Envy	Improve yourself or your life, get others to be fair, devalue others' possessions, avoid them	Avoid destroying others' stuff, count your blessings
Jealousy	Protect what you have, leave the relationship, work at being more desirable/fight for them	Let go of control of others, share with others, don't spy, don't avoid

Continued ➤

EMOTION	URGE/ACTION (IF JUSTIFIED)	OPPOSITE ACTION
Love	Be with the person, touch, hold, embrace, avoid separations, fight for them	Avoid the person, distract from thoughts of them, avoid contact, remind yourself why love isn't justified
Sadness	Grieve, retrieve/replace what's lost, rebuild, ABCs (page 110), ask for and accept help	Get active/moving, avoid avoiding, build mastery, fully engage in pleasant events
Shame	Hide what's rejectable, appease others, change, avoid those who disapprove, find new people	Reveal your characteristics to people who won't reject you, repeat without hiding, apologize and repair (if justified), forgive yourself
Guilt	Seek forgiveness, make amends, repair damage, accept consequences, commit to change	Do the thing you feel guilty about (if guilt is not justified), make it public, find new social group

What is the opposite action for the urge I identified in the previous exercise?

What specific ways can I do this opposite action in my situation?

Act Opposite 110 Percent

Opposite action is one of those "what you put into it is what you'll get out of it" situations. If we only sort of do opposite action, we will only sort of get results. Perhaps we go to the party and stand off to the side, only talking to people we already know well. We might feel a little less nervous, but we likely won't walk away feeling confident and capable. However, if we confidently walk in with our head high and speak to everyone there, looking people in the eye and smiling, having conversations and acting confident, it will have a much greater result.

GOING ALL THE WAY

Identify your all-the-way opposite action for the scenario you've been working with. Continuing from the opposite action you identified in the last exercise, how can you take that opposite action even further? Do the opposite action, and repeat if necessary. Then do it again. And again.

What is my all-the-way opposite action?

How did I feel after doing it?

How would I rate my original emotion out of 100 now?

Continue to Practice Acting Opposite until the Emotion or Urge Subsides

Continue opposite action at least as long as it takes for the emotion or urge to start to come down at least a little bit. If you leave the situation before the emotion comes down, you may reinforce the association with the emotion that doesn't fit the facts. Continuing until the emotion shifts is how you make new connections in your brain and teach it that it's okay to let the emotion subside.

It's important to keep practicing opposite action, even when it's challenging. Sometimes it works right away, while other times it requires repetition. Try not to go down the path of thinking *This isn't working*, just because change is not always immediate. That is the opposite of the confidence we need for full opposite action.

PRACTICE THE POSTURE

Practice the physical posture that is the opposite of urges for at least three different emotions. Write about how it feels in your journal.

KEY TAKEAWAYS ....

In this chapter, we covered two major categories in regulating our emotions. First, we learned that one of the most effective ways to be more resilient and less likely to get overwhelmed or overwrought is to live a life that feels meaningful and worthwhile. The other category of ways to reduce vulnerability has to do with balancing our physical equilibrium. Having a body that is as balanced as it can be means that we are less likely to get blindsided by big emotions.

The other half of this chapter focused on skills for reducing big emotions once they've already arrived. We learned about identifying our emotions, checking the facts, and doing opposite action.

Our emotional patterns have been with us for a long time. It is not easy to change them, but I promise it is possible.

Key points from this chapter:

▶ Having a life that you find worthwhile is what will keep you moving forward.

▶ The ABC PLEASE skills will be your best friends and will set you up for success.

▶ Emotions are important and suppressing them will just make them bigger.

▶ Opposite action is science—your body can convince your mind that it's going to be okay.

Understanding Your Wants and Needs with Interpersonal Effectiveness

It is okay to ask for what we need, and it's okay to say no.

In this chapter, we will learn a bit about the challenges that go along with communicating effectively, including big emotions and the patterns that sometimes come along with them. We will also think through how to determine our priorities in any given interaction.

Finally, we will focus on being able to ask for what we need or to say no to requests in relationships. We will begin to learn some of the core interpersonal effectiveness skills that give us the ability to get what we need, keep our relationships, and maintain our self-respect.

WHAT IS INTERPERSONAL EFFECTIVENESS?

The interpersonal effectiveness skills in DBT, as stated earlier, aim to help us balance our goals, our relationships, and our self-respect. They are broken up into three categories that I'll describe here briefly. We will focus on the first category over the next three weeks: building the core skills needed to achieve your goal or objective in any given interaction while still maintaining the relationship and your self-respect. These core skills provide a foundation for all interpersonal interactions, including the other two categories: finding and keeping relationships and ending destructive ones; and walking the middle path, or balancing acceptance and change in relationships. We don't have space for those last two categories in this book, but they are important concepts to consider as you continue to build positive relationships as part of your life worth living.

How Emotions and Relationships Interact

As we discussed in week 8, there can be a complicated interaction between interpersonal distress and emotional distress. So what does this mean for learning interpersonal skills?

First, it means that if we have some challenges in the way that we relate and communicate, and our emotions ramp up and make it messy, we are not alone. It's not uncommon that folks with BPD or other patterns of big emotions get told they are manipulative or demanding. Terms like *passive-aggressive* are thrown around, or they're described as *too intense*. When you consider that people with these patterns have spent a lifetime being misunderstood at best and often outright criticized for the way they express their emotions or relate to others, it's not surprising that their interpersonal skills and confidence may need some improvement. Common patterns like controlling, lying, blaming, threatening, being overly intense, being dependent, and sliding between idealization ("You're perfect and wonderful") and devaluation ("You're worthless and I'm done with you") keep people in loops of chaotic relationships because that's all they know.

Remember that we seek to understand the function of these behaviors and why they developed, not to judge people for using them to survive.

The skills we are about to learn are focused on giving us new tools for getting what we want or need in all kinds of relationships, not just romantic ones, without sacrificing the relationship or our self-respect.

CLARIFYING YOUR PRIORITY

When you are interacting with a person and either asking for something or saying no to a request they've made, it's important to know what your priority is for the interaction. Think of a current, upcoming, or recent interaction in your life. I've given some examples in the following list. Write down your situation(s) in the lines provided. Next, decide which of these three priorities (Objective/Goal, Relationship, and Self-Respect) is most important in this moment and write that down. In the next three weeks, we will spend more time clarifying what these priorities mean, so don't worry about getting it "right."

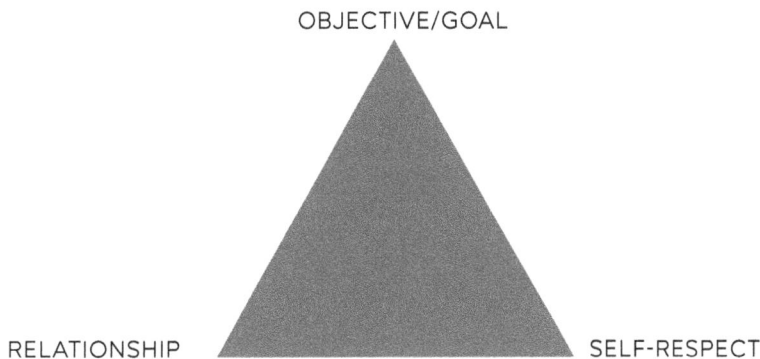

OBJECTIVE/GOAL

RELATIONSHIP   SELF-RESPECT

Situation

1. Buying milk at the store.
2. Asking for a raise.
3. Asking for a raise after five years.
4. Saying no to a person who frequently asks you to cover for them.
5. Saying no to a friend because you're sick.

Priority

1. Objective/Goal
2. Relationship with boss
3. Self-respect
4. Self-respect
5. Objective, maybe Relationship?

Situation

1. ....
2. ....
3. ....
4. ....
5. ....

Priority

1. ....
2. ....
3. ....
4. ....
5. ....

PRACTICING DEAR MAN

The DEAR MAN skills are guidelines for helping us be as effective as possible in getting our goal or objective, whether that is to ask for something or to say no to a request. They are also helpful when we are trying to stand our ground and maintain our stance on a topic. In later weeks, we will build on these with the

GIVE and FAST skills, which help us determine the tone we want to maintain, depending on our overall goal in the situation. Whether the goal is to protect the relationship or to maintain our self-respect, we will continue to use the foundational assertiveness skills of DEAR MAN.

When you put the four steps of DEAR together (describe, express, assert, and reinforce), you have a script for starting a conversation. We will use the examples from the previous exercise as we learn each step. I encourage you to stick to one situation you have identified in your own life as you do each of the practice exercises.

Describe

Just as we did in the mindfulness chapters, we will start by describing the situation. It's important to avoid judgments and only describe the facts. This orients the other person to your goal and gets both of you on the same page. As you try to decide which facts to include, emotions can sometimes make it tricky. Step back and think of what someone observing from the outside might see. When you describe, you aren't yet asking for anything. You are just introducing the topic. Some examples of the describe skill are below:

EXAMPLES OF DESCRIBE

Buying milk at the store: *"I need to buy some milk, please."*

Asking for a raise: *"I would like to ask for a raise in my pay."*

Asking for a raise after five years: *"I have been here for five years and have not received consistent raises when others have."*

Saying no to a person who frequently asks you to cover for them: *"I am not able to cover for you every week."*

Saying no to a friend because you're sick: *"I can't get together today because I'm sick."*

DESCRIBING THE SITUATION

Using the examples from the previous exercise, try writing your own describe statement. Try it a few times, focusing on just describing the basic facts of the situation without judgments or interpretations, and without making excuses or giving justifications for why you're asking or saying no.

_____

_____

_____

_____

_____

Express

Briefly express your feelings or beliefs about the situation. Telling the other person a little bit about your own reaction will help the other person understand what you are really asking for or why this is important to you. This can feel a little scary, but it's important for them to know where you are coming from. This can also feel like we are trying to be manipulative, but that's not what this is. We are simply letting people know what we are feeling and what is motivating us to communicate with them. Some examples of the express skill are on the following page:

EXAMPLES OF EXPRESS

Buying milk at the store: *"I'm concerned that my kids won't have enough."*

Asking for a raise: *"I believe that my job performance has earned it."*

Asking for a raise after five years: *"I feel that I should be valued accordingly as an employee since I work so hard and always show up."*

Saying no to a person who frequently asks you to cover for them: *"I already work a full week and am very tired from my own schedule."*

Saying no to a friend because you're sick: *"I hate to let you down."*

EXPRESSING YOUR FEELINGS

Add your "express" to your "describe" from the previous exercise in the space provided. Again, try two or three times to express what you are feeling as simply as possible without any finger-pointing or blaming.

Assert

To assert is to ask clearly for what you want, without hedging. Try to be as succinct and clear as you can. Don't expect the person to read your mind or figure out what you're asking for or saying no to, and don't make demands. Even if you feel you shouldn't have to ask, it's more effective to be clear. Be brave and say it. Being assertive not only makes what you are asking for clear but also increases your self-respect.

EXAMPLES OF ASSERT

Buying milk at the store: *"Can you ring up the milk for me?"*

Asking for a raise: *"Can you approve a raise?"*

Asking for a raise after five years: *"I am asking for you to give me a raise."*

Saying no to a person who frequently asks you to cover for them: *"I am not able to cover for you every week."*

Saying no to a friend because you're sick: *"I am not able to get together"* or *"Can we reschedule?"*

ASSERTING YOURSELF

Continuing with your scenarios, try writing several ways to assert yourself or clearly ask for what you're requesting in the space provided.

Reinforce

To reinforce is to highlight a benefit that the other person will gain if they give you what you're asking for. If you take a moment to consider your request from their perspective, you might be able to connect what you're asking for to what they need. This might be a natural effect of the situation, or it could be something you'll do for them, such as being a productive employee if they give you a raise.

It is generally far more motivating for people to receive rewards or positive consequences than threats of negative consequences.

EXAMPLES OF REINFORCE

Buying milk at the store: *"I appreciate your help and it makes me want to keep shopping here."*

Asking for a raise: *"A raise will help me want to keep working here."*

Asking for a raise after five years: *"A sufficient raise would help me feel valued, and I want to continue to contribute to this company."*

Saying no to a person who frequently asks you to cover for them: *"I would really appreciate it if you would ask other people sometimes."*

Saying no to a friend because you're sick: *"I will feel so much better knowing you're okay with rescheduling."*

REINFORCING OTHERS AND TYING IT ALL TOGETHER

Finally, write down some options for reinforcing the other person for working with your request.

_____

_____

_____

_____

Now go back and put your top choices all together:

D: _____

_____

E: _____

_____

A: _____

_____

R: _____

_____

Now you have your very own DEAR script.

(Stay) <u>M</u>indful

When you are presenting your DEAR script, there are some things to keep in mind. First, you want to keep your goal in mind and stay focused and on topic. Being mindful of your objective, try these techniques:

- ▶ Act like a broken record, continuing to repeat your request or say no over and over again. You can either start your DEAR again from the top or pick the part of it that is most important. Keep saying the exact same thing in a calm tone of voice. This will help you stay on topic, even when arguments or distractions are introduced by the other person.

- ▶ Ignore attacks and diversions. If the other person attempts to threaten, distract, attack, or throw you off, just continue to repeat your request. Don't get thrown off. Getting pulled into the diversion will make the person more likely to use that tactic again in the future.

BROKEN RECORD

It is hard to know what attacks or diversions might come up in a conversation. To prepare for this, think about the core of what you are asking for. Say we're using the example of asking for a raise. Perhaps our core, or the thing we most want our boss to hear, is "I really believe that I have earned a raise. Will you approve one?" That can be our broken record statement that we repeat if the boss is getting off track.

What is the core of what I'm asking for?

What are three different ways I can state it? Practice saying these out loud at least five times.

....

....

....

....

....

Appear Confident

Stand tall, hold your head high, and make eye contact (unless considered culturally disrespectful). Use your posture to communicate confidence and that you deserve respect. Don't whisper, stammer, fidget, act unsure, or back away. Note that it's okay if you don't necessarily *feel* confident. Act like it anyway.

PRACTICING CONFIDENCE

Once you have your DEAR script, practice it in front of the mirror. Notice your posture and facial expression. Write down anything you think might be a challenge and review it before you go into the situation.

Things to remember about my tone and appearance of confidence:

....

....

....

Negotiate

While it's important not to apologize or back off on your request, sometimes it's necessary to be willing to negotiate. Sometimes being willing to be flexible on less important details is okay if you still maintain the parts of the request that really matter to you. You might also suggest alternative ways to solve the problem or ask the other person for their thoughts on creative ways to solve the problem.

BE WILLING TO NEGOTIATE

Consider whether there is a compromise that you'd be willing to make while still getting the most important part of what you want, or whether you'd be willing to do something they're asking for but not all. Write down in the space provided what you'd be willing to offer to get what you really want while still maintaining the relationship and your self-respect.

Here are some ideas for ways to practice putting DEAR and MAN together:

- ► Write out your script and memorize it or keep it with you.
- ► Practice your script out loud.
- ► Practice in the mirror, adjusting your posture and practicing looking confident.
- ► Ask a friend or family member to help you practice. Have them be helpful and receptive once and then argumentative a different time.
- ► Ask a friend out to dinner or coffee.
- ► Ask an employee at a store for help finding something.
- ► Ask someone you don't know what time it is.
- ► Call and order food, and ask for customized options.

KEY TAKEAWAYS ....

You have now been introduced to the DEAR MAN skills, which form the foundation of the skills for being effective in our communication in all kinds of relationships. Since emotions can so often fuel our communications into ineffective territory, sticking to these skills can be crucial if we want to stay on track when we are either asking for something from another person, saying no to a request they've made, or trying to maintain our stance on an issue.

Key points from this chapter:

- ► We need to ask clearly for what we want or need as it increases our chances of getting it and also helps maintain our self-respect.
- ► Appearing confident helps communicate to others that we are deserving of respect.
- ► Sticking to the point is important.
- ► The more we practice these DEAR MAN skills, the more confident we will be in our ability to communicate effectively.

Strengthening Your Relationships Using Validation

Validation is simply acknowledging that our feelings and perspective make sense if we understand what led to them.

Last week, we learned about skills for reaching your objectives or goals in interactions with others in all kinds of relationships, whether that is to ask for something, say no to a request, or maintain your stance in an interaction with another person. Those skills, referred to as DEAR MAN, are also the foundation for interactions when we have different priorities. This week, we'll focus on how to validate when your first priority is to maintain the relationship with the person. It would be easy to think that if the relationship is the priority, then you just wouldn't push for your agenda or ask for anything. Ultimately, though, the relationship would be damaged over time if one person in the relationship never got what they needed. The goal is to be assertive while still being able to validate the other person's perspective and keeping or improving the relationship.

WHY IS VALIDATION IMPORTANT?

Validation can mean many different things, but in this context it means to recognize and acknowledge that the other person's perspective—feelings, thoughts, and actions—makes sense if you understand the background or context. Even if you disagree completely with a person, you can validate or acknowledge that they landed at their own perspective through their own experiences and that you see where they're coming from. Validation accomplishes several important things, including making our interactions with other people better, making us better communicators, and giving us opportunities to get closer to other people.

Invalidation Is Often Well-Meaning

People don't always mean to be invalidating. Sometimes they're trying to be encouraging and miss the mark. Other times they're just not in tune with what you're needing. It's possible to validate that they're doing the best they can while also acknowledging that their invalidation is hurtful. There are things you can do to recover from hurtful invalidation, whether it was intentional or not. You can:

- Be mindful of your responses: thoughts, feelings, and body sensations.
- Catch yourself turning the invalidation into negative self-talk and cut it off; keep a log and challenge the thoughts.
- Acknowledge that your responses are valid.
- Tell someone supportive about how it felt; if you're up to it, ask how they would've responded in your shoes.
- Tell yourself it isn't the end of the world.
- Remind yourself that their behavior is caused by their history.
- Work on changing your unskillful responses.
- Check the facts and run through the situation with someone you trust.
- Be compassionate toward yourself, on purpose, frequently.

REWRITING YOUR RESPONSES

Think of a time when someone said something that hurt you a little bit. I'm going to walk you through identifying how it affected you, how you responded, and more skillful ways in which you can respond. Rewriting our own negative self-talk and being compassionate toward ourselves reminds our bodies and brains that we don't have to believe the invalidating things people say. We are forming new, self-validating pathways in our brains when we use these various techniques. Follow these prompts:

Situation/what they said: ....

....

....

....

Your responses (thoughts, feelings, sensations): ....

....

....

....

Negative self-talk you turned it into: ....

....

....

....

Write a challenge for the negative self-talk: ....

....

....

....

Reflect on doing something compassionate for yourself:

....

....

....

....

LINEHAN'S SIX METHODS OF VALIDATION

Way back in chapter 1, we talked about dialectics. We learned that the main dialectic in DBT is acceptance and change, or validation and change. We learned Linehan's primary reason for including validation in DBT: to balance the focus on change. When people are asked to shift and change, it is easy for that to make them feel like they're not okay, or not valid, the way they are. However, when people are validated—when they feel seen and valued—at the same time that they are being asked to make changes, it balances the request for change.

Linehan's second reason for incorporating validation into DBT was the recognition that when we validate others, they can use that example to learn to validate themselves. Clearly, these dynamics will look different in therapy than in our other relationships, but they are still important. Validation not only improves our communication and interactions, but also it provides an environment in which other people can feel the freedom or safety to let down their defenses, thereby being more open to connecting, cooperating, and communicating with us. This is not manipulation; it's being effective or doing what works.

In no particular order, Linehan has given us six different ways to validate other people.

Pay Attention

Being fully present with another person goes a long way toward validating them. People can tell when you are present with them and it lets them know you're interested and that what they're saying matters. Turn off the TV, put down your book or phone, and don't multitask. Make eye contact and really listen. Or just sit with them. Be sure your body language or facial expressions aren't unintentionally communicating invalidation. Paying attention or being present doesn't mean we agree with everything a person is saying. It just means we are hearing them and acknowledging their perspective.

DEEP LISTENING

Sit with a person you know or are getting to know. Ask them a question and really listen to their response. Make eye contact, subtly lean toward them while they're talking, and don't fidget. Put your phone away and don't even look at it. Later, record your experiences in your notebook, noting how the interaction went, how it felt to pay full attention to this person, and how they seemed to respond. Try not to be thinking about what you're going to say next, or what you're going to write in your journal, while you're listening to the person.

Reflect Back

In this skill, you want to let the person know that you have truly heard what they are saying. At appropriate moments without interrupting, you might say, "I hear that you are really upset," or you might repeat a small part of what they've said. Your goal is to let them know that you have heard the words they're saying and that you're also picking up on the emotions they're feeling. This can be tricky and may take some practice as it's important not to add your own interpretations or assumptions to the mix. It's also key to be open to being wrong and to not get defensive if you try to reflect back and you don't quite get it right.

Again, you aren't agreeing with the person. You are just letting them know you hear them.

BE PRESENT

Practice this skill with a friend or family member, or even a therapist. Ask them to talk about something they're experiencing. Try to pick up on and reflect back on a couple of these things:

- ▸ The parts of the story that seem important to them (e.g., "It sounds like it was a busy and stressful day and your boss was making demands").

- The emotions they're expressing (e.g., "I hear that you're feeling stressed and tired and maybe unappreciated").
- Their hopes, wishes, or frustrations (e.g., "Sounds like you could use some encouragement that you're doing a good job").

Remember to be open to getting it wrong. If your comments don't seem to land, gently ask, "What am I missing?"

Read Minds

Reading minds is sometimes an expansion or deepening of the previous skill, reflecting back. In reading minds, you are considering what you know about the context, what you see of their affect, expression, body language, how people generally respond to such events (e.g., a death in the family), and your knowledge of the person. From there, you're taking a leap, making an educated guess at what they might be feeling. Having someone else guess at what you're feeling without having to say it can be extremely encouraging and validating. However, we can easily get it wrong. As such, it's important to:

- Suggest your thoughts tentatively. Don't present them as though you're telling the person what they feel.
- Be cautious and open to getting it wrong. Don't assume you know their feelings or intent.

Note: As we discussed in mindfulness, we can never know for sure what another person is thinking or feeling unless they tell us. We also cannot expect other people to know what we are thinking or feeling unless we tell them. This level of validation is simply meant to show that we are listening well enough to make some connections and care enough to try to understand what they're telling us. We are always open to being told our guesses aren't quite hitting the mark.

MIND READING REFLECTION

Consider a time when someone else either didn't take your feelings into consideration and made a decision that affected you, or a time when someone seemed to assume (incorrectly) they knew what you thought or felt. Think about what that felt like for you and write down some ideas in the space provided on how they could have gone about it in a different, more effective way. Consider how you could incorporate these ideas into how you approach validating people with mind reading.

_____

_____

_____

_____

_____

Understand Their History

The goal of this type of validation is to let people know you see how their responses, thoughts, feelings, and actions make sense given their history and experiences. This suggests an understanding that everything has a cause. A person's history or wiring can easily lead to certain responses. For example, a person with health issues might get tired easily, or a person with a history of scary or traumatic experiences might not respond well to surprises. A person who lives in a rainy place is likely to carry an umbrella, while a person with limited access to food might be less likely to throw even small portions away.

Note: Acknowledging that certain responses are caused by past experiences does not mean those responses are fixed or unchangeable. Even if we've been responding a certain way for a very long time, we can still learn new ways of responding.

UNDERSTANDING A PERSON IN THEIR CONTEXT

Think of someone you know well. Try to think of some characteristic responses they have. Can you tie their unique responses or ways of functioning back to experiences they've had or unique features of who they are? Write down your ideas. Then consider some of the ways you respond to situations yourself and see if you can make sense of them in this way.

_____

_____

_____

_____

_____

Acknowledge the Valid

While it is powerful to be validated based on your own history, it is even more powerful to be validated because your response is categorically or universally valid—or it fits the facts across the board. Validating a person by saying that their feelings make sense and "anybody would feel that way in your shoes" is powerful; acting out that validation makes it even more powerful. Imagine someone says to you, "It's really frustrating for me when you block in my car when you know I have to leave for work super early in the morning." If instead of saying, "Why don't you just grab my keys and move my car?" (invalidating), you say, "You know what? You're right. I didn't think of how inconvenient that would be. I'll move my car right now and make sure not to do that again" (validating). You've just doubly validated their perspective by acknowledging _and_ solving the problem.

UNDERSTANDING TYPICAL HUMAN RESPONSES

Think of times when you've felt empathy, sympathy, or compassion for other people, relating to how bad they must feel and imagining how you'd feel similarly if you were in the same situation. Write down some situations that have made you feel this way on the lines provided. Then write down what you could say or do that the person might experience as validating. Note: It is not always appropriate or necessary to solve others' problems for them just because you want to validate them.

Example:

Situation: *Co-worker has sick child at home*

What I can say or do: *"Wow, you must be worried. Why don't you go home and I'll close up tonight?"*

Situation: ....

....

What I can say or do: ....

....

....

Situation: ....

What I can say or do: ....

....

....

Situation: ....

....

What I can say or do: ....

....

....

....

Show Equality/Radical Genuineness

Be present, be real, and show your honest responses. As DBT therapists, this is a big one. Rather than having stereotypical, calm, "therapist-y" responses, DBT therapists are known for just showing their genuine reactions to things our clients share with us. You can do this in many relationships in your life as well. Showing people that you see yourself as their equal rather than separate from or superior to them can make them feel validated.

RADICAL GENUINENESS AND BEING REAL

Can you think of a person in your life who has treated you as an equal who could have acted superior to you? Who in your life can you do the same for? Write down some ideas for how you can treat people you see in the course of your regular life as equals, including friends, family, co-workers, classmates, service workers, and public employees. See if you can make someone's day by "seeing" them. Be sure to record your experiences and return to them later to remember what the experience was like.

....

....

....

KEY TAKEAWAYS

Validation is a key component of not only DBT but also of any relationships that we want to keep and improve. Relationships are hard and require change and work, and validation is crucial to balance that hard work. It also allows us to encourage others and ourselves, and it creates room for us to be vulnerable and take risks. Without vulnerability and risk, there can't be closeness and intimacy. Linehan gave us six different ways to practice validating other people, as some of us haven't had much experience validating or being validated. We can recover from painful invalidation and learn to validate ourselves and others.

Key points from this chapter:

▸ Validation isn't agreement; it's just seeing people.

▸ You don't have to accept invalidation from other people when they're wrong.

▸ You can learn to validate yourself by acknowledging your own feelings, reframing self-criticism, getting support from friends, and being kind to yourself.

▸ Being genuine and valuing other people's genuineness are two of the most powerful ways to validate.

Becoming a Better Communicator with Interpersonal Effectiveness

Relationships and self-respect go together;
it's hard to have one without the other.

In week 10, we covered the DEAR MAN skills, otherwise known as skills for objective (goal) effectiveness. DEAR MAN guides us in coming up with language and tone that increase our chances of success in asking for and getting what we need, or saying no to someone else's request. It's also useful for maintaining our position or stance in a discussion.

DEAR MAN also provides the foundation for discussion when we have different priorities, such as strengthening the relationship or maintaining our self-respect. When our priority is to maintain or strengthen the relationship, we add the GIVE skills, which focus our approach on validating the other person. If self-respect is our priority, our tone and manner are guided by the FAST skills, which assure that we will feel good about the way we handled things after the interaction is done. We will learn and practice GIVE and FAST in this chapter.

STRENGTHENING RELATIONSHIPS USING GIVE

The acronym GIVE ([be] Gentle, [act] Interested, Validate, and [use an] Easy manner) is the skill we add to DEAR MAN when our priority is relationship effectiveness, or when what is most important to us is protecting the relationship while also getting our objective met. The question we might ask if this is our priority is "How do I want the other person to feel about me after this interaction? And is that more important than getting what I want?" In using the GIVE skills, we are increasing the chances of both things happening: We get what we want *and* the person likes or respects us as much or more than they did before the interaction.

Similar to the MAN skills, these are more about the tone in which we communicate than what we actually say, though the words are also important.

Note: We cannot always make the relationship the priority. It can be scary to risk rejection or disapproval, but if we always sacrifice our personal needs or wants to keep the peace, the relationship will eventually become so unbalanced that it can't continue. We must balance short-term goals (peace and harmony) with long-term goals (health and balance for both people).

(Be) Gentle

Be respectful, kind, and not harsh in your tone and style. Avoid threats, disrespect, judging, and verbal attacks. Expressing direct anger on the regular doesn't tend to make people want to be around you. Any overt or hidden threats to get your way should also be avoided—they might get someone to give in for the moment, but they don't work long term. Try to stay present even when it's painful or you don't get what you hoped for. Also, stay away from name-calling, put-downs, expressions of scorn, and guilt trips. Watch for judging and, as in mindfulness, try to observe and describe problems without judgments, interpretations, or insisting you know their intent. There are times to point out problems, but even that can be done in a respectful and gentle manner. Just state the facts.

Note: If there are dangerous dynamics at play or you are trying to leave a harmful relationship, please seek professional support and guidance. Check the Resources section on page 164.

(Act) Interested

If you want someone to hear your point of view, do the same for them. Take an interest in their opinions and perspective. Expect a discussion to be two-sided, and show interest in their reasons for disagreeing or saying no, if that's their perspective. Don't assume you know what they're thinking. Ask. Listen to their answers. Don't interrupt or talk over them. Be patient and willing to have the conversation at a different time if that's what they need.

In reality, you may not always be interested in what someone has to say, and that's okay. You can still choose to listen because it matters to them, and letting them know they matter will move you toward a positive relationship.

Validate

We covered validation at length last week, but it's so important for keeping and improving our relationships that we'll reiterate it here. Relationships aren't about just getting what we want; they're about interacting and connecting with the other person in whatever ways fit our roles with each other. We validate the other person so they know we understand where they're coming from. It doesn't mean we necessarily agree or share the same viewpoint. We can validate *why* they feel a certain way while still not agreeing with *what* they think or feel. For example, we can understand why they're losing their temper while wanting them to find a different way to express it.

When we're validating, it's most effective to use words as well as tone, posture, facial expressions, and actions.

(Use an) Easy Manner

Finally, when we are focused on improving or maintaining the relationship, it helps to use an easy manner. If we can smile, use humor, and keep things light, it helps our requests go over a little smoother. Diplomacy and soothing emotions can reduce tension and defensiveness. No one wants to be pushed or bullied into cooperating. Making people feel good about working with you is an important skill. You can do this while still respecting and validating their perspective.

USING GIVE

Return to your scenario from week 10. Consider how your DEAR MAN might be different if your priority were the relationship. Write down some things you could do if you were using GIVE in that situation.

G: ....

....

....

I: ....

....

....

V: ....

....

....

E: ....

....

....

MAINTAINING YOUR SELF-RESPECT USING FAST

The question to ask if your priority is self-respect effectiveness is "How do I want to feel about myself after the interaction is done?" The FAST skills ([be] Fair, [no] Apologies, Stick to your values, and [be] Truthful) are designed for when we want to feel good about the way we've handled ourselves when using DEAR MAN. Sometimes people feel they lose self-respect when they show "too much emotion," such as tears, nervousness, or anger. Others feel that way if they either give in easily or are demanding.

Self-respect is something we should try to maintain in every interaction, no matter our top priority. Often we've consistently leaned too far in either the direction of not protecting our self-respect at all or protecting it to the extreme. Our goal with the FAST skills is to both maintain our self-respect and to still be effective at getting what we're asking for.

(Be) Fair

It's important to be fair to both yourself and the other person. Taking advantage of people over time will chip away at your self-respect. On the flip side, if you consistently give in on what you want or need and let other people take advantage of you, your self-respect will also suffer. Balance sticking up for yourself and respecting other people's wishes.

(No) Apologies

Don't over-apologize. The urge to apologize for existing, taking up space, having an opinion, or asking for something is essentially never warranted. If you apologize for making a request, it implies that you are in the wrong for asking. This will chip away at your self-respect. It can also harm relationships to excessively apologize. Acting like you don't deserve to be there might just convince other people of that falsehood over time.

Note: If an apology is needed to repair the relationship, it is likely a different conversation. If you feel it needs to happen before your FAST conversation, write a separate script. If the apology is indeed the goal, then let the apology be specific and succinct rather than excessive.

Stick to Your Values

Know what matters to you and stick to it. This is not about rigidity; it's about living by your own values and morals. Sometimes there is conflict between the values of two people in a relationship. We sometimes have to choose whether to flex our values to maintain the relationship. You may at times feel that circumstances justify this. Know that over time consistently allowing your values to take a back seat can erode your self-respect and ultimately destroy a relationship. Consider how often your values get ignored. If it is more than an occasional occurrence, it will be important to give some attention to bolstering your self-respect in your interactions and making sure your values are guiding your actions.

(Be) Truthful

Being dishonest, even in small ways, can chip away at your self-respect. It might not seem important if you're getting what you want in the moment, but telling big or small lies, acting helpless when you're not, and exaggerating can all decrease your self-respect. Dishonesty and false helplessness are the opposite of building mastery, which we discussed in week 9.

If you've relied on forms of dishonesty to reduce conflict and discomfort in the past, there is no judgment. It probably helped you feel better or avoid difficulty for the moment. However, since our goal now is to be effective at maintaining our self-respect *and* our relationships, it is going to be important to move away from it, as it will chip away at both.

USING FAST

What are some things you have done that haven't helped your self-respect in your interactions with other people? What are some things you can try to improve these interactions? Returning to the scenario we picked up from week 10 in the GIVE exercise, how would you use each of the FAST skills if you are prioritizing self-respect in your situation?

F: ....

....

....

A: ....

....

....

S: ....

....

....

T: ....

....

....

COMBINING GIVE, FAST, AND DEAR MAN SKILLS

For relationships to be balanced, we need to consider what both parties need in our interactions. When we are asking for something for ourselves, we want to consider how the request is going to affect the other person. The reverse is also true. We also try to maintain self-respect all the time but not at the continued expense of our relationships or goals.

As we use DEAR MAN scripts to assert our wishes, we are rarely using GIVE or FAST to the exclusion of the other. It's both/and. When we are being firm with the FAST skills, it will go better if we do it in a gentle and validating way. The core of our request when balancing them might be:

▸ Asking for a raise after five years: *"I understand that the company's finances have been tight for the last few years, and it's also important to me that my contributions are recognized and rewarded."*
  or:

▸ Saying no to a person who frequently asks you to cover for them: *"I know you don't know the others very well and it can be intimidating to ask, but I really need you to ask someone besides me sometimes."*

GIVE AND FAST

Returning to our scenarios from week 10, how might you phrase your core request using both GIVE and FAST?

My bottom-line request/what I really want: ....

....

....

....

How I could phrase it using GIVE and FAST: ....

....

....

....

KEY TAKEAWAYS ....

In this final week together, we've learned the rest of the core interpersonal effectiveness skills. The GIVE skills are for when keeping or strengthening the relationship is the top priority. The FAST skills are for when maintaining self-respect is the top priority.

When it comes down to being effective in interacting with people, though, we will use both sets of skills in most contexts. Being gentle, interested, and validating is effective at connecting with people in most settings, especially when saying hard things. At the same time, being fair, not apologizing, sticking to values, and being truthful won't go wrong even when you're focused on being gentle. Building relationships that incorporate your values and goals, and treating yourself and others with respect, fairness, and validation are key parts of moving toward your life worth living.

Note: No matter how effectively or skillfully you communicate, things will not always go the way you're hoping. There are times when the environment or the other person is just not going to cooperate. However, in many, many interactions, these skills will increase the chances of things going well.

Key points from this week:

▸ Communicating effectively requires being clear about what you want.

▸ Communicating effectively requires practice.

▸ You can't force other people to cooperate, but you can increase your chances of getting what you want by communicating clearly.

▸ Interpersonal interactions will go better if you're functioning in wise mind—because wise mind, or balancing our reason and emotions, and feeling confident in our actions, is *always* our goal in DBT and in life.

The Next 12 Weeks and Beyond

As you look back at where we've traveled together for the last 12 weeks, I hope that you can see some progress and themes emerging. A workbook like this just skims the surface of DBT, but many of the most important components are represented here. These aren't disjointed concepts and random skills but rather a road map to set you on the path to your life worth living.

The skills are split into two main categories: skills to help you change things or solve problems that are in the way of your desired life, and skills to help you accept and tolerate the things that cannot change—or that cannot change right this moment. So often we end up repeating the patterns that we should change and refusing to accept things that we wish were different; the result is that we stay stuck in chaos and suffering.

Working through this book can help you identify the problematic ways you may have coped in the past, learn some new ways of coping, and begin to build your confidence in your ability to be skillful. I strongly encourage you to continue writing in your journal and to go through these skills and exercises again, as often as needed. Some, such as opposite action, mindfulness, willingness, and DEAR MAN, can be used on a daily basis. Others, like the crisis survival skills, are ideal for when you're in a truly difficult, temporary crisis. Yet others, like accumulating positives and building mastery, will be part of the long game as you move toward a life based on your own values and goals.

There is far more depth to be found in embracing a new, skillful way of living. Whether you pursue it on your own through other books or online resources, or you decide to find a DBT or other therapist, I sincerely hope you will find these skills and new ways of thinking to be life changing as they have been for so many.

Thank you for spending this time with me. I wish you well.

Resources

FINDING A DBT THERAPIST

Behavioral Tech, a Linehan Institute Training Company: BehavioralTech.org
/resources/find-a-therapist

DBT-Linehan Board of Certification: DBT-LBC.org/index.php?page=101163

Psychology Today: Search the "Find a Therapist" tool for DBT therapists in your
area. Ask about their training before scheduling an appointment. Psychology
Today.com/us/therapists

CRISIS HOTLINES

Crisis Text Line
Text 741741

National Domestic Violence Hotline
1-800-799-SAFE (7233)
TTY 1-800-787-3224
SMS: Text START to 88788

National Sexual Assault Hotline—RAINN
1-800-656-HOPE (4673)

National Suicide Prevention Lifeline
1-800-273-TALK (8255)

The Trevor Project (LGBTQ Support)
1-866-488-7386

Trans Lifeline
US: 1-877-565-8860
Canada: 1-877-330-6366

WEBSITES

Behavioral Tech—A Linehan Institute Training Company: BehavioralTech.com

DBT Self Help: DBTSelfHelp.com

DBT Self Help on Reddit: Reddit.com/r/dbtselfhelp

The Family Connections Program: BorderlinePersonalityDisorder.org/family-connections

"Learning to Celebrate Neurodiversity in Mindfulness" article: Mindful.org/learning-to-celebrate-neurodiversity-in-mindfulness

Now Matters Now: nowmattersnow.org

PODCASTS FOR CLIENTS

DBT & Me: Open.Spotify.com/show/0q4Ri6Mc8npuq3qZk1ONRV

DBT Weekly: Podcasts.Apple.com/us/podcast/dbt-weekly/id1460055048

The Skillful Podcast: Podcasts.Apple.com/us/podcast/the-skillful-podcast/id1461774020

PODCASTS FOR THERAPISTS

To Hell and Back: CharlieSwenson.com/podcasts

YOUTUBE SERIES

DBT-RU: DBT skills are explained by Shireen Rizvi at Rutgers University. YouTube.com/channel/UC7lKAPBLpZzXk3AZbG_BAQQ

Linehan on DBT: YouTube.com/watch?v=Go8IYl2DAMg&list=PL_L7KEOxOeQ_gwUQX8ExtaIt3jSm8XYbK&t=0s

MEDITATION APPS

Calm: Calm.com
Headspace: Headspace.com
Insight Timer: InsightTimer.com
Waking Up: WakingUp.com

WORKBOOKS

DBT Skills for Teens with Anxiety by Atara Hiller

DBT Skills Training Handouts and Worksheets (Second Edition) by Marsha M. Linehan

The DBT Skills Workbook for Teens by Teen Thrive

The Dialectical Behavior Therapy Skills Workbook: Practical DBT Exercises for Learning Mindfulness, Interpersonal Effectiveness, Emotion Regulation, and Distress Tolerance by Matthew McKay, Jeffrey C. Wood, and Jeffrey Brantley

The Dialectical Behavior Therapy Skills Workbook for Shame by Alexander L. Chapman and Kim L. Gratz

The Expanded Dialectical Behavior Therapy Skills Training Manual: DBT for Self-Help, and Individual & Group Treatment Settings (Second Edition) by Lane Pederson and Cortney Pederson

The Neurodivergent Friendly Workbook of DBT Skills by Sonny Jane Wise

BOOKS FOR CLIENTS AND FAMILIES

DBT Skills Training Manual (Second Edition) by Marsha M. Linehan

Loving Someone with Borderline Personality Disorder: How to Keep Out-of-Control Emotions from Destroying Your Relationship by Shari Y. Manning

The Mindfulness Solution for Intense Emotions: Take Control of Borderline Personality Disorder with DBT by Cedar R. Koons

Trauma-Sensitive Mindfulness: Practices for Safe and Transformative Healing by David A. Treleaven

References

INTRODUCTION

"Core Evidence and Research." Behavioral Tech. Accessed December 1, 2021. behavioraltech.org/research/evidence.

CHAPTER 1

Linehan, Marsha M. *Cognitive-Behavioral Treatment of Borderline Personality Disorder*. New York: The Guilford Press, 1993.

Rathus, Jill H., and Alec L. Miller. *DBT Skills Manual for Adolescents*. New York: The Guilford Press, 2014.

Swenson, Charles R. *DBT Principles in Action: Acceptance, Change, and Dialectics*. New York: The Guilford Press, 2018.

CHAPTER 2

Chapman, Alexander L. "Dialectical Behavior Therapy: Current Indications and Unique Elements." *Psychiatry* 3, no. 9 (September 2006): 62–68. ncbi.nlm.nih .gov/pmc/articles/PMC2963469.

Collins, Nathan. "Mental Rehearsal Prepares Our Minds for Real-World Action, Stanford Researchers Find." Stanford News. February 15, 2018. news.stanford .edu/2018/02/15/mental-rehearsal-might-prepare-minds-action.

Dean, Jeremy. "Mental Practice Makes Perfect." *PsyBlog* (blog). March 5, 2013. spring.org.uk/2013/03/mental-practice-makes-perfect.php.

"RCT and Non-RCT Summaries." Behavioral Tech. Accessed October 21, 2021. behavioraltech.org/research/evidence.

Salsman, Nicholas L., and Marsha M. Linehan. "Dialectical-Behavioral Therapy for Borderline Personality Disorder." *Primary Psychiatry* 13, no. 5 (May 2006): 51–58. researchgate.net/publication/228693753_Dialectical-behavioral _therapy_for_borderline_personality_disorder.

WEEK 3

Greenland, Susan Kaiser. "A Mindfulness Practice to Notice the Mind-Body Connection." *Mindful.* August 7, 2019. mindful.org/a-mindfulness-practice-to -notice-the-mind-body-connection.

Mayo Clinic Staff. "Mindfulness Exercises." Mayo Clinic. September 15, 2020. mayoclinic.org/healthy-lifestyle/consumer-health/in-depth/mindfulness -exercises/art-20046356.

Mrazek, Michael D., Michael S. Franklin, Dawa Tarchin Phillips, Benjamin Baird, and Jonathan W. Schooler. "Mindfulness Training Improves Working Memory Capacity and GRE Performance While Reducing Mind Wandering." *Psychological Science* 24, no. 5 (May 2013): 776–81. doi.org/10.1177 /0956797612459659.

O'Brien, Melissa. "How to Use Mindfulness to Work with Difficult Emotions: A Six-Step Process." *Everyday Mindfulness* (blog). June 13, 2014. everyday-mindfulness.org/how-to-use-mindfulness-to-work-with-difficult -emotions-a-six-step-process.

WEEK 6

Kabat-Zinn, Jon. *Full Catastrophe Living: Using the Wisdom of Your Body and Mind to Face Stress, Pain, and Illness.* New York: Bantam Books, 2013.

Linehan, Marsha M. *DBT Skills Training Manual.* 2nd ed. New York: The Guilford Press, 2015.

WEEK 7

Robinson, Bryan E. "The 90-Second Rule That Builds Self-Control." *Psychology Today.* April 26, 2020. psychologytoday.com/ca/blog/the-right-mindset /202004/the-90-second-rule-builds-self-control.

"The Role of Emotion Regulation in DBT (Part 1)." Behavioral Tech. April 8, 2019. behavioraltech.org/role-of-emotion-regulation-dbt-part-1.

ADDITIONAL REFERENCES

Koerner, Kelly. *Doing Dialectical Behavior Therapy: A Practical Guide*. New York: The Guilford Press, 2011.

Linehan, Marsha M. *DBT Skills Training Handouts and Worksheets*. 2nd ed. New York: The Guilford Press, 2014.

McKay, Matthew, Jeffrey C. Wood, and Jeffrey Brantley. *The Dialectical Behavior Therapy Skills Workbook: Practical DBT Exercises for Learning Mindfulness, Interpersonal Effectiveness, Emotion Regulation, and Distress Tolerance*. Oakland, CA: New Harbinger Publications, 2019.

Pederson, Lane and Cortney Sidwell Pederson. *The Expanded Dialectical Behavior Therapy Skills Training Manual: DBT for Self-Help, and Individual & Group Treatment Settings*. 2nd ed. Eau Claire, WI: PESI Publishing & Media, 2020.

Index

NOTES

NOTES

NOTES

NOTES

NOTES

ACKNOWLEDGMENTS

My ability to put DBT into words wouldn't exist without the global DBT team. Their generosity and willingness to share knowledge and collaborate is nothing short of amazing. I also wouldn't be the therapist I am without my teams, past and present: Iain, Doc Melinda, Katie, Ann, Kim, Molly, Cameron, Jamie, and Britney, Dr. Susan L, Susan S-F, and David. Thank you for loaning me your insight and your words.

ABOUT THE AUTHOR

Valerie Dunn McBee, LCSW, is a native Midwesterner who lives, works, teaches, and worships in and around Athens, Georgia, with her husband, kids, and dog. She stumbled upon DBT circa 2007 and has never looked back. When not working, she's probably planning a trip, listening to an audiobook, knitting, attending a kids' sporting event, or swinging around on a trapeze. She's maddeningly dialectical in most things and answers too many questions with "It depends . . ."

www.ingramcontent.com/pod-product-compliance
Lightning Source LLC
Chambersburg PA
CBHW061236270326
41930CB00022B/3486